UEA UNDERGRADUATE ANTHOLOGY
2021-2022

CONTENTS —

8	**The Little House At The End of Tartarus**	Adam Webber
12	**Romance of the Mythical**	Aisla McKenzie
13	**Meadow Hare Presage**	Alice Cunningham
14	**Madagascan Sunset Moth**	Amber Juncal
15	**For Those Now Lost**	Andre Hughes
19	**Bramble-King**	Barnaby Hill
21	**Breakfast Rewind**	Cat Faux
22	**How it Gets In**	Cathy Sole
24	**Prescription Leaflet**	Charlotte Bouilloux
25	**Narcissus**	Chris Bowler
26	**Storm in a teacup**	Daisy Campbell
28	**Hanging On**	Denise Monroe
32	**Swear Upon the Hollywood Dream**	Diva Hemawani
36	**The Artist**	Elena Rodgers
40	**Embracing**	Elizabeth Yew

42	**NEW ADDRESS BOOK**	
	Ella Pamment	
47	**THE HUM**	
	Ellen Newall	
51	**SEASALT FOOTSTEPS**	
	Emma Mcdonald	
54	**JUST IN CASE**	
	Ersi Zevgoli	
58	**STARS AND STRIPES**	
	Esther Jardine	
59	**MAGNAPINNA**	
	Fin Doktor	
61	**I REMEMBER**	
	Freya Calcluth	
65	**PLEASE.**	
	Freya Calcluth	
66	**THE WAY I'LL DROWN**	
	Freya Calcluth	
67	**YOU TELL ME YOU LOVE ME**	
	Freya Calcluth	
68	**STEAK DINNER**	
	Georgia Greetham	
69	**CAPTAIN HOOK WORKS NIGHTS**	
	Grace Bartle	
73	**MELTED LOLLIES**	
	Grace Bartle	
74	**TELL ME YOUR FANTASIES**	
	Ingrid Jensen	
75	**SHE SAID THERE'S A SCORPION IN ME**	
	Jennifer Shen	

77	**The Chicken Dance** Jessica Blissitt	
78	**You took our peace away** Julian Beacom	
81	**Off the Radar** Kathy Floyd	
85	**THE ANGEL** Kyle Wakefield	
88	**THE DEVIL** Kyle Wakefield	
89	**The Not Garden** Kyleigh Taylor	
91	**The Butcher of Belarus** Laurel Brown	
93	**Love is a Hot and Cold War** Lidia Lassed	
96	**03:11** Lily Fitzgerald	
97	**bury me in the creek** Lucy Cundill	
98	**Claire** Lucy McEleney	
99	**Tuscan Sun** Maddy Hadwin Donnelly	
101	**Frog** Magda de Soissons-Page	
104	**Genesis, Today** Maya Elphick	
105	**The Yellow Room** Megan Dennison	

106	**The World Ends** Mia Galanti
110	**Convenience** Mica Magsanoc
115	**All Saint's Eve** Ollie Briggs
116	**Bodies** Paloma Parás Ochoa
119	**Isolde** Paloma Parás Ochoa
122	**Cascade** Robbie Tyler
125	**Birthday pt.2** Rowena Price
126	**Sometime, Illumination** Rowena Price
127	**Toy Horse** Seb Lloyd
129	**Back To Us** Sophie Wallwin
138	**One Million Nerves** **Synne Solbrekken**
139	**Under the Artist's Loving Eye** **Thomas Smith**
143	**The other side of the lake** **Tianyu Zhou**
147	**A Matter of Perspective** **Victoria Her**

Note from the Editors—

2022 marks the ninth annual publication of UEA's Creative Writing Anthology and the sixth year that Egg Box, UEA's publishing society, has had the honour of bringing it to print. This year also represents the largest collection of student work Egg Box has published to date, a feat we have managed without compromising the quality of the prose, poetry, and script submitted to us by the undergraduate cohort of Creative Writing students. Though we return to those published in previous years, we also include debuts from UEA's freshest writers. We have thought of this collection both as an expression of homecoming and new beginnings; perennial crops re-emerging with a bounty more fruitful than the last, along with fresh displays of previously undiscovered talent.

Egg Box is unique in that it is both part of the UEA Publishing Project and functions as a UEA society. From its inception, the mission has long been to demystify the process of publishing and to serve as the first step on new writers' publication journeys. Through working with our society members and the students on UEA's Creative Writing course, we are proud to produce collections of work that demonstrate not only the supreme creativity of UEA's students, but their enduring perseverance and dedication to the craft. The past two years have exemplified these qualities and can be seen in the previous two collections of student work that we have published. This year's, however, celebrates a coming together of writers from every corner of the world. As Norwich has welcomed back its far-flung writers, scattered by the pandemic, this UNESCO city of literature has started up again in earnest. In recognition of their contribution to our wonderful city's thriving literary scene, you can find this year's included authors' biographies at the back of this book.

The standard of work in this anthology is truly spectacular, but it is more than the collected efforts of our writers that make Underground the stunning collection it is. We must thank each team that worked on the anthology's creation; the editors, marketers, and launch coordinators. We want to say thank you additionally to Anna Brewster for her stunning design work, as well as Philip Langeskov and Nathan Hamilton for their guidance in bringing the anthology to print. Thanks also to the school of Literature, Drama and Creative writing, whose opportunities and pastoral care have allowed every creative writer to flourish in their own right.

There were fears initially that submission numbers would be low; that motivation to sit and write would have been dampened by the storm persisting over the last few years. And yet, you hold in your hands the indisputable proof that the writerly spirit is one of the most enduring. We invite you into a multitude of worlds, feelings and experiences in the following pages, and hope that you enjoy exploring the writings of UEA's budding talent as much as we enjoyed collecting it.

All the best, and happy reading,
The Egg Box Editors

The Little House At The End of Tartarus
Adam Webber

One of my favorite things to do is wake up. Younger, I used to take it for granted, then I moved here. One may call it a town.

Most of the activities happening here in Tartarus are out of your control. The only thing that's really in your control is waking up. My friends tell me it's not true. They tell me they decide to get dressed and come to the town hall where we play card games all night, with brief breaks in between for our nicotine needs.

That's not true. I mean, they are right. They do get the message and they do choose not to ignore it, but if they do ignore it nothing will really happen. If I decide not to wake up tomorrow, my life will be in shambles for the next 24 hours. I might be able to fix it after that. Nothing guaranteed though.

If I choose not to wake up tomorrow, next month's phone bill will show a number starting with 01, not 00.

01 calls to 00 aren't unusual. 01 calls to 00 mean something is fucked up.

The sun shines straight through the curtains I forgot to close last night. I see them, and I think it over. Will it be worth it this morning? All I'll lose is five hours of my life. Then security will come and- I'd rather not tell you what it is they'll do if I decide not to wake up. It's not because it's brutal and I want to spare you, but because I actually don't know. There are many rumors, well they're called rumors, I see them more as myths, as to what they do to you between those five hours. I would rather not lie to you.

After staring at the light infiltrating my sleep, I decide to open my eyes. I stretch while sitting on the side of my bed and grab my nicotine sticks from my bedside table drawer. I light one and smoke about half of it while waiting for the coffee I put on. I don't drink all the coffee either.

On Wednesdays, at the town hall, they serve us fruit salad for breakfast. I get dressed, a shirt, not the white one. The white one has a bolognese stain from pasta fridays. I wear the green one instead, with the red threads down the inside, not the one with the blue threads down the outside. My shoes are plain white, and my trousers are white with purple splashes, as if the manufacturers were opting for a "bleached" style.

Once I'm at the town hall I sit beside Ary and his plate of fried chicken and salad. He's one of the ones we call the "conditioned", there's nothing really wrong with him, he just gets really anxious if he doesn't eat chicken at every meal. Security tends to his needs just as well as they tend to all needs of the "conditioned".

"Hi," I say.

He smiles at me, his teeth stuffed with a piece of chicken he's eating.

"How are you this morning, Tahona?"

"Happy, got to look at the sun for a bit." I don't tell him I considered not waking up, we've tried to have the conversation before, it doesn't ever go anywhere.

"I'm happy too."

"What did Dolce tell you?"

"We probably won't be seeing that much of each other anymore." He pauses. I know he hasn't finished, he just stuffs his teeth with a leaf of cos lettuce. "It was his decision," he says, "but I woke up today and found myself agreeing with it."

"You're not sad?" We don't use words like 'depressed' here in this town, not because they're too brutal but because we don't believe in the meaning behind it. We don't use "euphoric" either. Same reasoning.

"No. It's for the best.

We sit in silence for a bit as a group of people walk in and sit at our table. We both turn to them and smile, but we don't take the conversion any further. A waiter brings me my fruit salad and bowls of honey, lemon juice, yogurt, granola and a glass of blueberry smoothie on a clean tray. I thank him.

"Have you heard of your *mama*?" Ary asks.

"No. Should I have?"

"I think I saw her earlier on. Speaking with Donovan."

"Oh," I try to keep my voice smooth, but it hiccups, "how did she look?"

"Not too bad."

I eat my fruit.

"Are you okay?" Ary whispers

I nod, not because my voice would tremble, but because my mouth is full of grapes. Ary doesn't mind, we don't really ask if we're okay in this town, we could get in trouble if we're caught asking or replying.

I guess my friends are right. Maybe they're talking about that as they play cards. I'm not there. I stayed home, reading a book I bought at the shops yesterday. Donovan wrote it. I'm only eighty pages in but I'm really enjoying it. He named it "*The Little House At The End of Tartarus*".

Last night I stayed up past three in the morning reading the book. Donovan really outdid himself, I'll try and look for him today, offer him my personal congratulations. I won't ask him about my *mama*.

I didn't really miss much at the card games. Security came later in the night, as they changed shifts. They brought carrot cake. I'm not that big a fan of it, and the book was tremendous so I don't mind. ~

Ary, Li, Carmen, Jack and I joined the mountain walk. We packed some bacon and egg sandwiches, and some cigarettes for the road. The guides provided the water. We met by the town hall, where we had lunch. It was ham, cheese and spinach pancakes for everyone apart from Ary, his were chicken spinach and mushroom sauce.

We went out near the edge of the town, we stopped at the benches at the top of our mountain, which, while nice, doesn't compare to those we were sightseeing. There was a layer of snow at the top of the mountain though, we tried to make a snowman but to no avail.

I talked to them about Donovan's book on the way back, when I mentioned his name Ary shot me a glance, to ask me whether I was okay. Obviously he didn't actually voice it, while I trust Li, Carmen and Jack with my life, I don't with Ary's routine.

I heard the news of my *mama* coming and quickly forgot to care about it. I've been so invested in Donovan's work these past few days. I've been going to the different themed nights at the town hall, but apart from that, I close myself off with my books in my room. Ary came over last night and I lent him *The Little House At The End Of Tartarus*, he wanted to read it. He asked me whether I was okay. I didn't mention my *mama*.

It came as a bit of a surprise then, today, after meeting Li in the early afternoon for a cigarette and some lunch, Donovan came to me and told me I had to come with him.

I smiled at Donovan, unable to finish my cigarette, I gave Li a kiss on the cheek instead. He smiled at me as I followed the writer. He took me to the top floor of the town hall and into the restricted area. I'd *never* seen the place before, it was much nicer in natural light than the rest of the town hall. When we got to room 06, at the end of the corridor, Donovan opened the door for me.

Mama is waiting as I walk in. She has a cigarette she rolled herself unraveling in between her fingers. When she sees me, she stands up.

"Tahona."

"*Mama*."

"Sit down, *mija*, please."

I do as is asked of me.

"How have you been?" I say.

"Lonely." She tries to hold my hand, I let her. "It's been difficult not having you there with me."

"I moved out at 18, *mama*. I'm 37 now, at some point you're going to have to accept it."

Tears are already glittering in her eyes.

"What would you say if I asked you to come back with me?"

Silence looms over us. I stand up and grab a glass and pour it full with water.

"Why?"

"I'm preparing everything, mija. Tomorrow, we can both leave *together*."

"Why do you want me to come keep you company? What about Maria, have you asked her yet? I spoke to her a few days ago, she said she was having a few issues adjusting to life out of university."

"No, *mija*. Maria passed away from a stroke five years ago."

I'm having a cigarette with Ary at the town hall. It looks different now that I've been to the restricted area.

"Are you okay?" I ask him.

He looks up from his cigarette and hugs me tightly.

"Are you okay?" he says.

"No."

Asking if someone is okay is prohibited and punished. Answering is even worse.

My *mama* is holding my hand, she takes me down roads I've never come down. I have a cigarette on my ear and one, lit, in my mouth. We're following Donovan. He released a new book which I was the first to buy and read yesterday. It's called *The Phone Bill*.

They take me into this room, my *mama* isn't here anymore, just me and Donovan. He tries to make me speak but I've been feeling lightheaded ever since I came in. I'm starting to feel my eyelids close, and instead of fighting back, as I would have done, I just let it take me. I can hear Donovan's voice, I can't understand what he's saying. I just nod my head, I would not be able to choose whether to wake up right now, I have lost that power. I can't even choose to stay awake.

I feel different. It's been decided by Donovan and *mama* that I will be going back to help her for a few days, see how I'm feeling. Then I can come back. I didn't say goodbye to my friends, *mama* will only need me for a few days. I'm eating a chicken wrap as Donovan walks up to me.

"I really liked your books," I say.

He smiles, acknowledging my words.

Mama brings the car over and opens the door. I look at Donovan.

"Are you okay?" he says.

"No. You?"

He scratches his head. "I might be tomorrow."

I nod at him, I can't help but cry a bit. I turn around and get in the car with *mama*. As soon as I'm in I fall asleep.

Mama wakes me up. We're about to leave town. Security checks our car and papers and we're let through. I'm not really present, I realize I was woken up, I was not aware in my sleep. I have lost all control of my life.

Security clears us and *mama* drives away. I take a last look at the town and realize a sign at the top of the security desk.

TARTARUS
HOME FOR THE CLINICALLY INSANE

ROMANCE OF THE MYTHICAL
Aisla Mckenzie

She was a winged sprite. Her feathers changed with the weather and the scenery but always boasted mystery and strength. With wingspan wider than the world's embrace, she scraped the skies and skimmed the seas in one fell swoop. Her freedom was an essential ingredient.

He was a hybrid element. With the composites of an electric volcano and a breezeless summer eve. He was senseless and sensational. His hands cracked the solid sediment, and pulsing havens of rock, stone, and the purest of energies rose from beneath his fingertips. He lived for the current of the overwhelming, be it pain or passion.

They first met when the lightning from the earth and the sky reached out for each other in exultation. Her wings were the heaviest black from the rain, and his imposing structures sizzled noisily beneath her. She passed him at the speed of sound. He passed her at the speed of light. Each specs caught in the others' eye.

They met again on the sunlit peaks of a cliff face. He was busy creating the Earth's pulse. His eyes gave the sky its colour, and his arms produced a year's worth of weather. She was busy creating the Earth's beauty. Her tail sliced waves into the shore, and her wings lent vibrancy to the flowers. They watched each other work in admiration.

They finally collided on the night when the constellations danced among the treetops. They found each other hidden amongst the ancient oaks. She had shed her feathers for the solstice. He had become flesh for the full moon. They danced in mortality amongst the moonlight speckled forest floor.

MEADOW HARE PRESAGE
Alice Cunningham

If
You see
The meadow hare
Be sure to watch out
For a trick, they'll ensnare
You in a tangle of roots;
Bramble, barley, brush and bandersfoot.
Cheeky in nature yet good in omen,
They'll have you sure that they're a burden,
But stop, don't reach for your sharpened stick,
For hares are nothing if not frighteningly quick,
Instead speak a spell to keep them far and distanced from
Your precious home way up on the hill, oh so quiet and oh so still,
Then watch and sigh as you realise that without the hare there is no meadow,
Without the meadow there is no lark, without the lark there is no morning, and take
These words as a fellow warning; to disturb the world around you still, with magic, mischief
or just one spell, Will cause the pattern of our natural world to shift and shake and slowly
break into a million separate pieces of hell.
And I should know, for listen here
I too once was the
Meadow Hare.

MADAGASCAN SUNSET MOTH
Amber Juncal

I go for a walk because I miss my friends, though they are with me every day. A rainbow collapses across the hospital stretcher blue sky. The stranger and I both stop on Alexandra Road to stare at it. We might breathe the same Norwich air, but it will not taste the same. For me, it is a bittersweet medicine. A latex rubber glove investigating my teeth. An inescapable aftertaste. The stranger and I both move on with our days and I still miss my friends and they are still with me every day. Their papier-mache white limbs are inseparable, even by operation. The closeness of their bodies create an echo chamber for their laughter, which slips through the cracks in the floorboards and penetrates the peace in my bedroom. When did I start staying in bed for this long? Sometimes I have to be high to be home, stumbling through the hallway, vision rolling between a dimly lit mahogany hallway and a clinic corridor painted pale yellow to make patients patient. I don't need a doctor to diagnose this problem. It isn't the physical bodies, but the people they used to be inside. The friends I miss are missing. Their insides are missing. And they are with me every day. They are the wilting flowers in the sage green vase on the kitchen table. They are but aren't the faces smiling at me from the magnets on the fridge. I want to, have to get away. But they are with me every day. I don't remember spending this much time in bed. When the summer rolls around, my window is wide open and my rainbow fairy lights are forgetfully left on. The moth infestation upstairs becomes a painful reminder that change is just a part of life.

FOR THOSE NOW LOST
Andre Hughes

In the hallway after breakfast, I kiss your hair as you grab your coat off the hook rail. Pulling your arms into the sleeves, you zip the front to guard against the Autumn wind.

As I encircle your slender form, you tilt your head back against my chest; you smile, a gentle shrug, pushing ahead through the porch.

The door shuts behind you, the deadbolt scraping into the strike box.

I take hold of the oak volute, slide my right hand along its speech-mark and follow the breeze you let in up the handrail; the Grecian balusters shaking in their sockets.

It's my fault we left London with only leftover fridge items to nourish our souls.

On the landing I carry on past the study and the bathroom; my navy dressing gown rustles on the carpet as I turn.

You should be able to find the essentials in town, though there are no supermarkets.

I pause at the foot of the next staircase, on the breath-mark curled under the handrail. Stepping in common time to the bedrooms; my dressing gown rubs snare-like on the steps as my feet beat a steady oaken march.

Closely resembling my memory palace of when I was brought up here, the top floor consists of my room to the left of the corridor, my sister's to the right, and my parents' room at the back of the house.

A few years ago, Papa split his room into the guest bedroom and his bedroom.

We'd chosen to stay in the new guest bedroom, the one with my mother's dressing table against the side wall, because it's quieter and I don't recognise the view of the garden from the window.

The new wooden door doesn't creak as it opens onto the soft marron carpet, and I kneel by my side of the bed to rummage in my suitcase.

The light blue art deco armchair by the window is stiff as I try to settle into it, opening The Invisible Man on pages 164 and 165.

I read; *but now he was joined by another figure, a younger figure, myself—*

"Damn Solid All Along!" says a stocky male builder on a ladder outside.

"Really?" says Papa, tilting forward I see him looking up from the garden: I'm unseen.

I read; *They reminded me fleetingly of prisoners carrying their leg irons as they escaped from a chain gang. Yet they seemed aware of some self-importance—*

"Bloody high up," he mutters under breath, before rotating his head to state, "Solid Moss Not A Budge."

I read; *Maybe they got paid well for this, maybe they were chained to money—*

"Ah? What about further up?"

"No, Pointless!" he says to Papa, before saying to Mr White-Rendering "Need a spaceship to get higher than this, might fall off."

I read; *I had been told post offices were guarded, by men who looked down at you through peep holes in the ceiling and walls—*

Clack-clack, the bird song backing singers are joined by Ladder hitting against

House as he comes down from the sky.

I read; *to the right I could make out the statue of Liberty, her torch almost lost in the fog—*

"Three years ago, it happened. I just heard a sound like someone had tried to punch through wood."

"Humanity isn't it," he says, chatting to Papa in the garden, "Could happen to all of us."

"Thirty years, then suddenly she's gone. I wasn't able to say goodbye to her," Papa chimes in.

"You had a good load of time though. Thirty years," he whistles, "Don't happen so often anymore."

"Yes, it doesn't happen often, what with divorce being so common," Papa says.

"Mad world isn't it," he concludes.

Especially in here, I think.

Papa must have taken the Santander to Plymouth Brittany Ferries and come to oversee some building work on the way back home. He doesn't trust English builders, only French ones.

He'd stayed a few days here before spending his Summer along the west French Coast; Quimper, Le Sable D'olonne, Bayonne. And yes, he'd told me in August, calling from Le Sable D'olonne, that he'd booked a builder to look at the drainpipes.

Aah Ladder's building to the finale; the builder's back with heavy-duty gloves, white hard hat, hi-vis vest, and a bucket and scoop clenched in a fist to the sky. Sigh: I abandon my reading, shut the curtains, and get changed.

"It's the type of pipe that's open at the top and closed at the bottom," Papa tells me, after letting himself in for a tisane.

"It wasn't just full of moss and leaves, and other such matters that find themselves stuck in a drainpipe; a roof slate came out as well."

I listen, but I personally find it helps to block off the circulation of water from draining out of the system.

He'd only noticed it when it rained; all the water would fall onto the bay window.

"You could hardly think when in the living room," he says.

How heavy rain could be, I think.

As he continues, I mull over how I've got myself in this situation.

—Last week, knocking on Chief's office and putting my head through the door: "Have you got a moment?"

Glancing from her screen, she gestures to take a seat in front of her desk, "How can I help?"

"I need to take leave for a few weeks," I say.

"Oh, is everything ok?" she asks, opening the second desk drawer and taking out a binder.

"Everything's fine; it's just that next week is my mother's anniversary."

"I see. It's been a few years now hasn't it?" she says sympathetically, "Is the family having a get together? A family often becomes closer after death."

"My Fiancé and I are going to the family holiday home in south Devon."

"That sounds nice. It'll do you both some good, I'm sure," she says, showing me a sheet with a graph listing the Newspaper's employees. "You're in luck. You haven't used any of your leave this year."

"I prefer to get the off-peak prices."

She smiles and hands over a form. As I sign, she says, "I hope everything goes well next week, and there's no need to worry about the Music section, it's secure; I'm sure Max will agree to take over for the time you're gone."

I thank Chief for her understanding, but as I open the door, I notice that the yearly sales sheet has been left on the cabinet so as not to disturb her. I wonder, for who is it secure?—

"Small country towns soak everything up like a sponge," Papa says.

As if I didn't know that already. Of course, I think of newcomers as raspberry ripples in a crème onglés. Who wouldn't?!

"Îles flottantes," Papa says, floating islands. "Do you remember the last time I had one?"

I remember; he ordered it at 'Le lafayette' when we were on one of our many holidays in Les Sable d'olonne. I was twelve.

"It was ex-quisite!" he says.

He'd had another on his trip, the same restaurant as I remembered, but I don't tell him so. Instead, nodding my head and making an agreeing sound, I picture those white paper clouds drifting across the crème onglés: floating cities in the sky.

"There was hardly a ripple," Papa says, "on the Britany Ferries crossing to Roscoff. It was as flat as a milk pond out there!"

In contrast, I remember one of the family holidays on the same crossing. He'd said the same thing as a choking gurgle sounded in my head. The rolling of my dinner back onto the plate.

We're walking arm-in-arm up the main high-street towards the sea, the after-lunch light crossing the road with us as we pass the green grocers with the faded dark signs.

The owner, you say, doesn't remember what his shop's called, let alone what his prices are. You like his Braeburns, he gave you a good price.

Past the town shop joined at the waist with Royal Mail, you say, cheap milk, no alcohol.

We pass the two pubs; The Happy Farmers, The Knights Pilgrimage; one a dilapidated smoking den tattooed with dart boards, the other like smelly-dogs and even stronger pints. They haven't changed since I was young; same buildings, same signs, different owners.

As we walk, in the corner of my eye you seem to drift besides me. Though my two feet shuffle along the tarmac, my mind itches a stagnant rash.

—I'm still brushing crumbs off the kitchen table from our last family lunch, swiping pencil-round edge into a cupped left palm and dropping them into the stainless-steel sink. Morsels of bread, hummus, and other sandwich fillings tumble onto the laminate beige diamonds, bonding to my feet, merging with the dark woven dining room rug: an absent abyss—

On the corner of a house by a side alley, a plaque reminds me that the street, like many medieval towns, was where a fire broke out in a bakery; roads weren't as wide then and the fire brought the main high street down with it. I read about it in a book I found in the townhall yesterday afternoon. It reminds me of a similar book a local retired wannabe-historian wrote when I was a kid, the same title but a different cover, a similar fire, like a half-brother.

At the crest of the hill, where fenced-thatch and small leaded windows give way for the hedgebanks to begin again, I peer back the way we've come. The houses on both sides of the road roll down the hill and back up the next, obscuring my line of sight. The shadows of bulky overhangs, shifting overlapping bodies, linger in the height of the sun.

I turn on my heels; our interlocking arms are brought closer together.

—I find myself sat in a sit-up on my police-strobe blue, polyester, tufted-loop pile carpet.

Needles arrest my head; a numb turning pain.

I don't notice the shouting, only the silence that comes after, and the comfortable thickness of the four white pebble-plastered walls of my childhood bedroom. An easy thickness that relies on being old, not young, cold, not sung, stone, not sticks—

I do not notice that I am standing still until a whip of fresh air wraps a gentle hug, gone in a hurry to follow the headline further down. Leaving cold, star-like remnants in my head; hay-fever scarfs wrapping themselves around my sinuses, but the sneeze never comes.

You tug at my arm, and we carry on our walk.

An inflection from beginning to end, Maman's words didn't matter, just the way they were voiced: "When are you going to change the wallpaper, it's flaking handfuls. The stairs is more paper than wood!"

The sounds behind them give a clearer picture.

We'd heard the words before, though this time, they drop, twisting and turning, and strangle in her throat.

Three years ago today, the sky was like floating breadsticks dipped in Maman's bitter-dark ghastly marmalade; honey-toughened amber.

Twisting and turning in bed last night, I dream of leaning on my childhood windowsill and looking out at a starlit sky. I wonder how the sky can seem so empty when the stars are so bright.

I think we all dream at some time or other, of a starlit sky from our windows.

We can't always do so. Half of every day the sky seems empty of stars. We don't dream every night.

Most mornings I have porridge and fruit for breakfast, but today I have toast and strawberry jam, because that's what Maman always made for me.

I think that the sky is empty, because it's empty of someone like me.

She at the very least would have hoped. I can see her telling me so, smiling the only way she could: larger than life. I see her arms wrap me into a hug. She's holding me so tight that I can't think.

BRAMBLE-KING
Barnaby Hill

Bramble-king,
Small cadaver who sits
And writes his bible in ivy round his feet,
Spiders' webs wrap
Your rigor-mortis smile,
Did you know we'd do the same?
Tell us our fortunes, King of Brambles,
As evening dew stammers through the undergrowth,
Tell us what you see on the underside of
Your skull, now your eyes are sunken there,
Crowned with the plump opals of blackberries,
Catching five o'clock light.
What will happen at six?
Does it hurt that your hessian sashes,
Velveteen with mould,
Feast and fester between your ribs,
The forest mice trapezing into their homes
There, Bramble-king?
A black rat snake, mottled like fire smoke on the midnight,
Has taken the eggs from the nest at your heart,
So it is empty
Except for the scratchings of flora and fauna
As dead as you but nowhere near as alive,
And eternal,
And captivating when the light graces your
Bone-white sternum and turns our eyes to
Glimmering water and Something Else
    Breaks
Forth,
And what is it?
Why is your throne a blackened char,
Reaching up to the firmament,
Starred with twists of thorns,
And the taste of decay and thunderstorms?
Stairways of mushroom florets,
Leading to your regal knee,
A hand, bejewelled with moss and rain
Resting there, mildewy,
And the mud in Massachusetts never tasted so sweet
As when our foreheads kissed it and we devoured the

Soil that had relished your ruin,
Rich with electric lights and liquid flesh
And fungi that will steal our tongues as
We chew it in our mouths,
So we can speak your words,
Bramble King.
Our moms and dads don't know about here.
They'd never understand.
They would say the pinecone perfumes and jewels of amber sap
Are a waste.
But the bramble fruits aren't poisonous
They're in the folklore field guide
Vincent's big brother brings,
When he comes to the forest to See God.
But we've already found you.

BREAKFAST REWIND
Cat Faux

Leave me, honey,
when you're about to stick, don't
use your butter like a lifeline,
yellow like the clouds. You always
said we were cement, cracks coloured
solid, stuck into stone: a legend
of love through serpentine eyes, frozen
into flesh, soft and singing,
I ached for you that day, heart leaking
red jam. The presenter on the radio told me
it was breakfast, so I feasted on
love. When you left for work
I was cold. The spread turned to
                    stone, my toast became rock,
                                   I was cold. The spread turned to
                                   love. When you left for work
                                  it was breakfast, so I feasted on
                            red jam. The presenter on the radio told me
                              I ached for you that day, heart leaking
                                  into flesh, soft and singing
                            of love through serpentine eyes, frozen
                              solid, stuck into stone: a legend
                            said we were cement, cracks coloured
                              yellow like the clouds. You always
                                use your butter like a lifeline
                              when you're about to stick, don't
                                      leave me, honey.

HOW IT GETS IN
Cathy Sole

A baby cried in her mother's arms, and the mother cried with her. She came ten days early. She was a big baby and a big child. Unlike her brother, who'd been kicked out of the womb a month prematurely. Things were going to be different for this baby. This baby was strong. She was the loudest crier at the hospital; she had no fears of being told to shut up. She screamed and screamed as if she was trying to force her diaphragm to fly from her mouth and onto the hospital floor. The other mothers were jealous. They hid it behind veils of annoyance. This baby was a survivor, unlike her mother. She would go through life kicking and screaming and end up winning, despite where she came from.

But a mother, no matter how proud, can only tolerate so much kicking and screaming. Mother and baby had to take a bus back home from the hospital. All of mother's boyfriend's possessions were gone from her flat. Mother was alone with something that didn't care about her sleeping—didn't care for anything at all other than the constant need to scream. Mother began to find it hard to get out of bed. She saw no point most days; she wanted to lie still until she turned to dust, taking the baby into oblivion with her. But she always got up. She fed her child. She kept her clean. She washed her clothes. She ran the bath. She lived on benefits and food bank donations. She started to smell, and her hair went unwashed. She stayed in the same jumper and tracksuit bottoms for weeks at a time. But baby was always fresh. Mother used essential oils on her; baby smelt like vanilla and talc. She bathed her every other day, cleaned her nappies, powdered her bum, dressed her in sweet second-hand playsuits. She had everything mother could want for herself. And yet she wouldn't stop screaming.

Baby sucked the life out of mother. As mother grew weaker and weaker, baby's screams grew stronger and stronger. Until one day, ex-boyfriend came back to see baby. Mother wouldn't open the door beyond the latch. Ex-boyfriend brought baby clothes, nappies, milk, and money from his job with him, along with the chance for mother to sleep again. But mother refused to let him in; she was afraid for baby. She didn't want baby to suffer in the same way she had. So she shut the door. Let him pound at it with his fists. Let him call her names. Let him threaten her life, until he finally went away, taking his money and his love with him.

Mother sat with her back to the front door, sobbing into her hands as she listened to her screaming baby wail her guts up. She'd sacrificed all, but baby kept screaming. Mother went upstairs to look in the baby's crib. Baby's face was bright red with life and vitality. She was fat and sturdy. She was everything mother was not. She had taken all mother's life and given nothing in return. Mother picked her up, but baby screamed louder, splitting mother's eardrums until they rang out. She put baby down. "Stop crying," she said. Baby didn't listen. "Stop crying." She yelled, crying herself. "Stop crying." She yelled again, raising the flat of her hand and smacking it across baby's cheek.

Baby stopped crying.

Mother looked at baby. Baby looked at mother. Both had eyes full of fear and wonder. Mother looked at her hand; it was trembling. Baby breathed with her eyes wide open, terrified to make a sound.

Mother ran out of the room, tripping over the leg of her bed as she went. She slammed her bedroom door shut, ran out the front of the flat, and locked the door behind her. She lived above a Turkish corner shop on the nicotine-stained high street. On a clear day, she could see the sea from the front of the house. Mother saw it and, not for the first time, considered running in.

But in her hand, mother felt the sting of life throbbing. She felt existence in all its bitter violence pulsing through her fingertips. Reality, in all its sober crispness. It was a terrifying feeling; one she had not felt for years. Mother had to drown it, and did so by entering the corner shop, buying three bottles of merlot, and drinking herself into sprawled-out unconsciousness on her kitchen floor. She woke up with a headache, but she'd accomplished her mission: she had softened and blurred reality's hard edges.

She never let them get sharp again.
Baby stopped kicking and screaming.

PRESCRIPTION LEAFLET
Charlotte Bouilloux

WARNING—Some people taking antidepressants may feel worse before feeling better.
it's january and i'm still waiting for my time.
i wish for pink skyscrapers and affection,
Venlalic XL 150 mg prolonged-release tablet
is what i got instead.
the cold sweats, fever, and diarrhoea are worth it,
a sweet numbness replaces the hallucinatory pain.
colour theory helps me on my worst days;
sometimes i feel blue but that's better than black.
pink are my favourite days,
they make me forget the
WARNING—an increased risk of suicidal behaviour in young adults.
and the dark january that entails,
its colour brown.

NARCISSUS
Chris Bowler

He, long, flowing hair and eyes like a broken promise, wanders through the woods.
He, first light on a winter morning, picks his way over bent twigs and broken branches.
Narcissus, Narcissus, we called your name like a plea.
He, all silken skin with knives for teeth, stumbles into a clearing.
He, broken mirror twisted reflection, sees a pond, undisturbed, pure, ventures nearer.
Narcissus, Narcissus, we told you not to go without us, please.
But She.

She, new-born fawn, leaf in breeze, steps towards him, breaks her skin on broken branches.
She, reflection on rippling water, cries out but makes no sound.
But twig cracks speak for her, and
He, face like the smell of vanilla, turns.

She, eyes darting like a fly, searching for the window, stands frozen.
She, mouth of a puppet, strings on her fingers, twists his reflection against him.
See—can't you see him dancing in her eyes?
Narcissus, Narcissus, we tried to tell you but you wouldn't listen.

Now see again—She, eyes of water-lily, runs away, trips over bent twigs.
He, dark silhouette in the sun, alone again, bends to drink, and sees.
He, sees He.
Narcissus, Narcissus, Narcissus.

Now, look back—see He, white around yellow, bending by the pond forever.
See us, silver hairs curling to the ground beside him.
He, crouching, curving, bending, looks once and never leaves.

STORM IN A TEACUP
Daisy Campbell

I keep trying to make something out of the rain
dutifully gathered in the widowed teacup,

just something like the backbone of a seedling
or a place for a paintbrush to forget all it's done.

It's outside for birds to sip from; although too frail to handle
sprigs of wren feet, its blue glaze is learning silver from the tongue of a slug.

The water draws a chintz from the garnered grit of spring
across its once serene and unblemished face:

a pastiche of heaven, blotted with blossom,
pocked with a dull drowned fly in cruciform.

I am doubled doing double, now everything's inverted
as the cup stirs me whilst I snip at the lawn

wanton with its weaponised tufts of green,
lacerating water to a net of loose diamonds.

See, by morning, the sky's dropped soft clinging stars
which fade gently into earth as it colours it dark.

But the cat has a new saucer—the dog, the fireside chair.
And during tomorrow's walk, I'll be taking the lead

and I will see it as a kindness when the sky plants itself
into the ground, to be passively fractured by a child's boot.

And I'll wait for it to glaze over with composure,
as it subdues submerged storm clouds of silt.

And I'll stare whilst it's mottled with lucid slabs of sky,
killing simmering sunlight to graft a nimbus to a rock.

And I'll marvel at that depression in earth,
as it pastes a murmuration over the mulch.

And I'll watch as the dog laps paradise up
before the heat sends it drifting idly home.

And I'll liken it to this little frail curl of china,
which shrinks the world down to a circling sliver of sky

as it shrinks my world down to a little gold ring:
a sedimentary fortune in the base of my cup,

which is newly retired and abstaining from drink.
Because I keep trying to make something out of the rain.

HANGING ON
Denise Monroe

(extract)

Sarah put her cutlery on the table; she didn't feel like eating anymore. She knew they had to talk about him, that's why Claire had wanted this evening so much after all, but she wasn't sure she was ready for it yet. To her, Dad was scar tissue, a wound too deep to be picked at. Mike had said it wasn't normal to forget you had a living parent, but it had worked for her so far.

'So,' Claire's voice brightened as though nothing had happened. 'You know Mum's going to give me away at the wedding?'

'You're not thinking of asking Dad, are you?' Sarah's heart was really kicking now, but she managed to keep her voice steady.

'Oh, that would be good, wouldn't it?' Jo cackled. 'You don't know me Dad, but I'm your daughter and I'm getting married, and I wondered if you'll come over to England where you haven't been for fourteen years and give me away.'

Claire didn't laugh. Instead, she wound a strand of hair around her index finger and examined the split ends. 'We've booked our honeymoon in Australia.'

Sarah took a deep breath; she could see where this was going.

'Don't look so surprised. I was born there. We're going to have a blessing for Nan and Grandad and the cousins.'

'Well,' said Jo. 'I take it back. You have been busy planning.'

'I want to invite Dad.' Claire pushed her plate away, the food unfinished.

'No!' Sarah shouted, unable to contain her pounding heart any longer.

'Why not?' Claire's voice remained calm and controlled. 'He is my dad. Our dad.'

'Hardly.' Sarah's voice was loaded with bitterness. 'What's he ever done for us?'

'Look,' said Claire. 'I know this is difficult, but don't you ever think there might be more to it than we know?'

'What? Like Mum had a string of affairs and ran off with a barmaid and chose to stay on the other side of the world and never see her kids again?' Sarah was furious. Only minutes ago, she couldn't believe how lucky she was to have sisters. Now she wanted to punch Claire, smack her in the mouth, anything to make her stop. She wished she hadn't drunk so much.

'Sarah,' said Jo. 'It's alright.'

Sarah pulled the plate back towards her and pushed the potatoes around, leaving lips of congealed butter in their wake.

'It's just got me thinking,' Claire pressed on gently, as though to soften Sarah up. 'It feels that the time is right. A chance to meet him as a grown up and get to know him. I mean, if not now, then when?'

'Try never,' snapped Sarah.

Claire took her glasses off and polished them with the hem of her shirt. 'I know he was a crap dad, but he's the only one I've got, and I'd like to see him.' She put her glasses back on and sighed. 'I knew you'd be cross.'

'Damn right I'm cross. Is that why Jo had to be here? To protect you from me?' Sarah looked at Jo who had been unusually quiet. 'Well, say something then.'

Jo filled their glasses before speaking. 'I think it's a nice idea.'

That was not what Sarah was expecting to hear. She'd presumed that Jo would be on her side, see this was just Claire wanting to be the centre of attention, tell her to shut up so they could go back to talking about wedding dresses. 'In what way is it a good idea?' Sarah's voice was too loud, too hard, but she couldn't stop herself and turned all her anger onto Claire. 'Let me get this straight. You're going to tell Mum, not only that you're going on honeymoon to Australia, a place that she hates by the way, but that you're going to visit your long-lost dad, her bastard ex-husband, and play happy families? And you think she's going to be fine with that do you?'

'Sarah,' Jo reached across the table and touched her sister's hand.

'No.' Sarah snapped, pulling her hand away. 'You can't do that to her.'

'Hold on a minute,' said Claire. 'You're the one who insisted that we didn't invite her tonight, that it should just be us. You're happy enough to push her out when it suits you.'

'That's hardly the same, is it?'

'Can we all calm down please?' Jo drum rolled the top of the table, and her sisters slumped into their chairs. 'Thank you.' She cleared her throat dramatically and spoke to Claire. 'Now, I'm not against this idea, but it seems we're forgetting something.'

'And what would that be, oh oracle of all things?' Claire's sarcasm was becoming less subtle, and Sarah sensed the night slipping out of control. She wanted it to stop, but Jo kept talking.

'Dad. I mean, this whole argument would be a complete waste of time if he's not even going to turn up to your blessing, or whatever it is.' Jo leaned back in her chair and crossed her arms in front of her. 'Have you asked him?'

Claire twisted another piece of hair and tucked it behind her ear. 'Well, no. Not yet.'

'So, what makes you think he'll even show up?' Jo spoke kindly, and Sarah remembered when they were kids how it was always Jo who sorted out their squabbles because Mum was at work or doing the shopping or cooking their tea.

'Of course he'll show up,' Claire said. 'It's the blessing of his daughter's marriage.'

Sarah raised an eyebrow in the way that Dad used to. After he'd left, she'd spent a whole afternoon in front of the hall mirror training her left eyebrow to rise while her right eyebrow stayed static. Now it was a habit she couldn't undo even though she wanted to. 'Let me ask you something,' she said, as she tried to replicate Jo's calm.

'Sure,' said Claire.

'When was the last birthday card you got from Dad? One that he actually wrote?'

Claire didn't answer but chewed on a thumbnail and stared at the table.

'That doesn't prove anything,' said Jo. 'You should definitely ask him.'

'No,' Sarah felt the bubbling rage rise in her chest again as she tried to comprehend Claire's motives. 'It'll kill Mum.'

'It can't always be about Mum,' said Claire. 'I need to do what I want.'

'How can you be so stupid?' Sarah snapped. The injustice was too great, the selfishness too real for her to keep her rage in check any longer. She pushed herself up from her chair with such force that it crashed to the floor behind her. 'Can't you see he doesn't want to know us? He doesn't give a fuck and you're delusional if you think he cares even the tiniest bit about you.'

Jo reached for another cigarette and said nothing. Claire took her glasses off again and wiped her eyes.

'Oh, for fuck's sake,' Sarah spat the words out as though they were poisonous apple pips and ran out of the room, slamming the door behind her.

Sarah leaned over the sink and counted slowly to ten, just like she'd been told to. Her legs were shaking, and she feared she might cry. She opened a bottle of Perrier and reached behind the flour tin for her emergency pack of cigarettes, then snuck into the garden. It was a clear night, and the pole star flickered above her. She followed the line of stars that made the upside-down saucepan and remembered Mike telling her its name. It had been hard to hear his voice today, to remember that they had once planned for a future that now wouldn't happen. The frost in his voice had made her heart ache, and she shivered at the memory.

'I thought you'd given up,' Jo came into the garden wearing Sarah's favourite jumper. It suited her.

'Yeah, well, another thing I lied about.' Sarah offered Jo the packet. 'Want one?'

Jo took a cigarette and sat on the low wall next to her sister. The flame from the lighter flicked shadows across her face and Sarah thought she saw lines around Jo's eyes that hadn't been there before. They were getting older, and some things weren't changing.

'Why do we always end up talking about him?'

'He's part of us, I suppose.' Jo blew out a controlled stream of smoke. 'You know, Claire might have a point. Maybe it's time we faced up to it.'

'What exactly?'

'You know. Him. Leaving us. All that stuff. You can't tell me it doesn't bother you.'

'It did, but I got over it years ago. He left, it hurt, that's it. Done.'

Jo took another deep drag. 'Did you ever wonder why I left England?'

Sarah had never thought of that before, the reason Jo had gone to Spain. To her, Jo was always the glamorous and exciting one, the one Sarah wanted to be like, the one who did whatever she wanted regardless of the consequences. 'To get away from the weather?'

Jo choked on her cigarette smoke and spluttered a small cough. 'Well, there was that,' she chuckled. 'But no, it was to get away from Dad.'

'He wasn't even here.' Sarah was confused. After the divorce they had all come back to England, but not Dad. She hadn't even got to say goodbye properly, not that she minded. Not now anyway.

'I mean the stuff he left behind. I couldn't bear to be around Mum anymore. Watching her trying to cope, to get over him, move on. She was stuck in 1974, punishing herself for him leaving.'

'I never knew,' said Sarah. 'I just thought you wanted an adventure.'

'Yeah, well.' Jo threw her cigarette to the end of the garden where the tip glowed before slowly fading to grey.

'Are you sure there's nothing else bothering you?' Jo's voice was quiet, like the night around them. 'It just seemed a bit of an over-reaction in there. You seem a bit tense.'

'It's Mike,' said Sarah, finally ready to admit it. 'We're finished.'

'What? I thought he was away on a trip?'

'He is, but he's not coming back.'

'How can you not have told me?' Jo sounded shocked, like she couldn't make sense of what Sarah was saying and was trying to fix it in this new reality. Sarah didn't know how she felt; she still hadn't got it herself because it had happened so fast. She looked at the stars again, putting off the moment when she would have to speak, unsure if she'd be able to explain without cracking. She lowered her face into her hands and breathed in the smoky stink the cigarette had left on her. She really should quit properly. And then she said it, the words she'd been hiding for weeks. '*He wanted to marry me.*' That was all, just five words: He wanted to marry me. Nothing happened, nothing changed. The stars kept twinkling and, somewhere, Mike was still being Mike.

There was a pause and Sarah kept her head down. Although she couldn't see Jo's face, she knew the look she'd be giving her. That big sister, I'll look after you whatever you've done kind of face. Sarah sniffed and sat upright. 'I couldn't do it. I wanted to be able to say yes, but I just couldn't.' She gasped as she tried to contain her heartache, determined not to cry.

'We need to sort this,' Jo stood up and brushed the ash from her skirt. 'Can't you see, it's him that's fucking things up. Just cos Dad was an arse doesn't mean that all men are bastards.'

'Yeah, that's what my therapist said.'

'What? You've got a therapist? For fuck's sake, anything else you want to share?'

Sarah laughed despite herself, grateful for Jo and her ability to know what to say. 'No thanks. That'll do for now.'

SWEAR UPON THE HOLLYWOOD DREAM
Diva Hemawani

We started drifting apart at the same time we'd crossed our hearts and made a promise with the murky sky as our sole witness: *one day we will make it big together.*

Sometimes when I look back at it, I'd find myself wondering if the stars would've looked down on us and laughed had they been there.

But it's not as if I'd ever muster the courage to find out.

***

At sunrise, we began our chase after that grandiose dream of ours, in a beat-up car with a brand-new guitar sitting pretty in the passenger's seat. *Our baby*, you had once called it with a playful grin on your face. Then you asked if I would ever bestow a name upon the guitar (your words exactly), since it was my piggy bank that we'd destroyed for it. I'd never given you a concrete answer—only a nonchalant shrug and an empty, "I'll give it some thought one day. Maybe."

I—*we* never gave it a single thought ever since. That was how our first shared guitar got its name. Our baby, *Our Baby.*

In between corny lyrics about world peace, shitty chord progressions, and late-night talks about extraterrestrial life (or lack thereof), we'd tried to kill our road trip boredom by betting on our doom. You'd been so adamant that the car would die on us before we could reach Hollywood. I'd insisted that the engine would last—unlike the crumpled bills inside the pocket of your damaged jeans.

Here's the thing about being runaways with heads stuck in the clouds for too long: you start losing whatever common sense you might've had before.

We ended up stranded in the middle of nowhere the next morning, god knows how many miles away from our planned stop at Lakewood, Colorado. Come to think of it, we probably hadn't even been close to entering the state.

When the car came to a halt despite having a full tank, we grabbed Our Baby from the backseat, our bags from the trunk, and ditched the vehicle at the side of the road. You'd bid it farewell before we decided to go on foot. "Good riddance, you miserable thing!" Not once did we stop to look back at the car—it was something you'd stolen from your abusive dad, after all.

Good riddance indeed.

You'd told me that it felt liberating in a sense. "I don't know, it just feels like I can actually start anew this time." Your voice was unusually quiet. To this day, I still can't decipher the glint in your eyes before you slipped back into that usual happy-go-lucky demeanour of yours. "Anyway—"

You flashed me a shit-eating grin and held a creased twenty-dollar bill in front of my face.

"I win."

***

Somewhere in I-70, I came to realise that I'd probably known more about the bumpkin who'd taken us down to Lakewood than I'd known about you.

He'd asked about Our Baby once and gave us a sardonic comment about having the balls to leave home and sell our souls to the Hollywood devil, before going on a two-hour-long tangent about his questionable political stance. You'd warn me by giving my arm a gentle squeeze whenever I wanted to open my mouth to argue against it. *We need the ride,* had been written all over your face when you'd spared me a glance amidst your conversation with him.

I never asked what you'd actually thought of that bastard's words. This was why I'd never known anything about you beyond your passion for music and the existence of parallel universes.

Our next hitch had been a dandy middle-aged man who'd offered to take us all the way to Los Angeles. He was heading there anyway—said he wanted to pay his daughter a surprise visit, and that he hasn't seen her ever since her mother had divorced him. He'd told us that she was around our age, and the shiny guitar we'd carried around reminded him so much of her.

"I'm not asking for much," he'd said, "I'm driving you two all the way from Colorado—all I want in return is the guitar. You can find better ones once you get to Hollywood, I imagine."

I said, "We can't give up Our Baby," the same time you asked him to follow you to a nearby gas station for a *private chat*, leaving me alone for what felt like an eternity.

An ugly dark orange had started to emerge over the horizon by the time you returned, a thin layer of tears glistened your hollow eyes and teeth sunk into your swollen lips. The man had trailed along behind you. I wouldn't have caught the slight quirk on his lips in his otherwise neutral façade if the sun had completely set by then. He'd stopped in his tracks for a moment to pat my shoulder. "Keep the guitar, child," he'd told me, "I can see how the two of you are meant for Hollywood now."

Somewhere amid a terrain of canyons and forests, when he'd left us in the car for a bathroom break, I'd asked you what you'd done to him. It took me years to realise that I'd asked the wrong question. It wasn't you. It has *never* been you.

Not that you would answer me either way.

"Remember our bet?" was what you said instead, legs resting on the steering wheel and palms sandwiched between the headrest and the back of your head. "We haven't actually decided what we were gonna put at stake, have we?"

I shook my head.

"Well, I just thought of two things," you continued, "and I want you to swear to them, alright?"

I shrugged. "Shoot."

"The first one is to never, *ever* give up Our Baby."

Piece of cake, I'd thought. I nodded and waited for you to continue.

"And the second one—" Your gaze had been cast upon the same sky that had borne witness to our very first promise. We'd let silence fill in the air for a long moment, accompanying the musky perfume my mind had already begun to associate with the old man. Then you opened your mouth to speak again:

"The second one is to make it big in Hollywood for me."

I'd offered my hand for you to shake, but instead you placed your palm over it and lowered it down gently. A smile had adorned your visage, and despite the night reducing us into mere silhouettes, your eyes had twinkled brighter than the stars ever could. Then you leaned towards me with your head tilted to the right, warm breath tickling my skin as your eyelids began to close.

The next thing I'd registered was the unfamiliar sensation of your lips pressed against mine. I remember it vividly: it felt tentative, akin to a timid question rather than your usual bold statements. Vulnerable, unlike the front you'd always put up for the world.

We spent the rest of our days pretending like it never happened.

I still can't understand why you'd chosen to seal the promise with a kiss—nor do I know why *I* had to make it big in Hollywood *for you*. We were supposed to make it big together. That was part of the deal, wasn't it?

There are many things I didn't know about you—

—and even more that I still don't know about you.

***

There isn't much to say about our early days trying to make ends meet in Hollywood. Probably because it would sound too much like your typical rags-to-riches story, some A-listers would blabber about in interviews and whatnot. We'd coped with gruesome double shifts by saying that, at least we have something in common with the people we'd aspired to be.

We'd rented an apartment that was already cramped for one, let alone two (barely) grown adults plus one Our Baby. Then, when we'd saved enough for home studio equipment to start making demo tapes, we made a bet on how long we could last without going insane from the claustrophobia of having machines surround you. I told you that we'll be fine until next summer. You said that the inevitable seasonal depression of winter would bite us in the ass first.

Neither of us emerged as a winner. We ended up having to move out because we'd driven our neighbours mad first with our late-night jamming sessions.

***

The last fight in our nth shared apartment had started with me hitting the stop button a mere ten seconds into the song you'd spent weeks perfecting. I'd told you that it reeked of our amateur days in that faulty car. Said it sounded too much like the first song we'd ever written with Our Baby. *Trash*, as the producers would call it.

You'd been the first to break the silence—as always. The hurt in your voice had taken its sweet time to milk the regret out of my being. It had settled deep inside my memory alongside the ghost of your lips against mine, words and a myriad of emotions clashing against one another in a cacophony.

"When will I ever be good enough for you?"

After years of brutal rejections with a sprinkle of sketchy record deals, we'd agreed that it would be best to take a break from each other.

But you never came back.

***

We've always had a knack for turning the smallest things into a world of our own. That silly little dream of ours into a cross-country road trip, for instance. Petty arguments in our old homes into going our separate ways.

An awkward coincidental meeting downtown into a night-long reunion at the rooftop of our first apartment building.

At one point, you'd turned your head towards me and asked, "Don't you have a flight to catch tomorrow?"

"How'd you know?"

A burst of soft laughter drifted in the air. "Your tour dates aren't exactly what I'd call top-secret."

There'd been a faint twinkle amidst the haze and typical Los Angeles light pollution that night. I redirected my gaze towards it and only acknowledged you with a hum.

"You did it," you said. "You made it big in Hollywood."

"Listen—"

"I'm proud of you." And that had been enough for me to close my mouth. "I'm satisfied enough with what we both have right now. Wouldn't trade them for anything in the world."

I tried to ignore the blur spreading in my vision as I said, "Is this your way of saying goodbye?"

You'd only answered me with the diminuendo of your footsteps, your figure gradually disappearing into the darkness as you made your way down the staircase.

***

I wonder if you'd ever find out that I had eventually given up Our Baby.

I suppose that makes us equal now—we both have one promise we couldn't uphold in the end.

The guitar I traded it for still feels foreign in my grasp. The shimmer of its body when it hits the spotlight makes it akin to a blank canvas: pure, if not for the ruby red that recalls the glamour of the Hollywood dream. Clean, devoid of the traces of our bygone youth, if not a constant reminder of what we'd crossed our hearts to.

Even if it's only me ultimately standing alone, perhaps with the occasional glimpse of your shadow by my side—as if you're truly with me.

Maybe one day I will be content with it too.

THE ARTIST
Elena Rodgers

Glass panels with thin black frames frame the desolate ocean like a monumental painting. The waves lap against the shore; some jump when they collide with the jagged rocks in an attempt to escape the ruthless sea. Stark white lines cut through the soft navy sky and reach toward the verge. The building stands on the edge, toying with death, attempting to connect with the brutality of nature. An engine hushed as it rolled into the polished concrete drive, the headlights were killed as it stopped. The slick gun metal Lamborghini was silenced, and a black figure stepped out of the vehicle. The system clicked as access was granted to enter. He stepped inside and flicked the light on. The room was vast, it became one with the expanse of the sea beyond. With few walls, there was no place to hide. The spotless black marble counter overlooked the framed image of the sea; an expensive masterpiece of nature which he adored more than anything.

Gliding across the polished stone floor, the man moved toward the carved wooden throne at the head of the dining table and took his seat. Crafted out of a single pane of glass, the table overlooked and mirrored the darkness of the sea beyond. A woman drifted toward him, placing a rough piece of slate decorated with an array of food before him. Dinner was Mauritian Octopus Salad, which consisted of poached and charred octopus tentacles, fennel, onion and tomato salad with a mango fluid gel accompanying it. She straightened the napkin beside the slate before pouring him a glass of champagne. It was Monday, and he always had champagne on Mondays. The woman did not sit with him, rather she returned to the kitchen and wiped the surfaces again and again until the moon reflected off as brightly as it shone outside. When he had finished, she collected his plate, packing it away in the dishwasher before pouring him another glass of champagne. He stood before her, waiting. Briskly, she pressed her lips against his sharp cheekbone before adjusting his grey pocket square. She stepped back and allowed him to pass. He took a seat on the blood red armchair with golden feet and sipped his champagne in front of the simmering fire. She watched on for a moment in envy, before heading for her evening soak.

Leisurely, she drifted toward the bathroom. The floor was cold under her naked feet leaving warm imprints on the surface; echoes of her movements through the house left on the grey stone. The lock clicked softly as the tall wooden door disappeared into the wall, like a coin between a magician's fingers. The room stretched toward the window: a thin black rim framing the leaves beyond. There was a mirror which covered the left wall which she paused in front of. There was a scar carved into her right temple which faded as it travelled down her face. Her dull brown hair did not invoke images of women bathing under waterfalls like those of shampoo advertisements; rather ones of scurrying creatures seeking solace under floorboards. Luckily, there was something in her eyes which distracted from her vanilla hair. An intensity, a fire waiting to be ignited, which entranced all who met her. Engrossed with her reflection, she ran her finger over the top of her eyelid smudging the faded grey eyeshadow. Seemingly bored with the reflection staring back at her, the woman opened a lower cabinet and removed a brown leather bag filled with make up. There were creases in the leather of the ageing holdall which once housed her paintbrushes. Her husband loathed it. In fact, he thought she had given it away years ago. He did not know it lived in the cupboard under the mirror in their sleek bathroom, right beneath his nose. She smiled, the spark flickering in her eyes. From her bag, she removed two pencils; one red and one black. Beginning with red, the woman contoured the valley beneath her eyebrow. On her lower eyelid, she drew a black line which continued toward the other. These two lines did not meet. Her eyelid resembled a Rothko painting. Her face was its own convoluted portrait; a surrealist Picasso incongruously pieced together. She could exhibit herself in an art gallery:

The Artist.
2021

Description: A lonely creature making impressions of the world.

Her paintings were hung internationally in the most illustrious galleries, yet she craved more. She had not found the *pièce de résistance* which would place her name above all others. The work of art that would make her more famous than Dali, more famous than Monet, more famous than Van Gogh. She wanted to be known for redefining what art can be and how it comes into being. She looked down at her hands, the source through which her creativity flowed, and wished for that inspiration. She watched her bones move like the strings of a piano or the metal which joins the key to the imprint of a typewriter. They mesmerised her. She followed them as they floated through the air toward the golden bath taps, bathing in the waterfall which began to fill the grey bath with hot water. Her palms were soft, like an unused paintbrush, and when she ran her thumb across her left palm she could feel every bristle. The wind arose outside, whistling to her. She looked up from the map of her hand to the window which framed a man.

His black hair was saturated from the relentless downpour. The statue watched as her fingers teased at the ribbons which held her dress together revealing the unmarked skin below: a blank canvas waiting to be painted upon. Slowly, she slid her hand beneath the strap and let it slip down her shoulder. She had lost control of herself since her marriage. Here she reclaimed her body. The garment fell to the floor leaving her nude in front of this stranger. She dipped her right hand into the bath; her matte black nails were distorted by the water. She lowered her body allowing the still waters to embrace her. Inhaling peaches, which transported her to the rolling hills of Fuyang, where pink trees lean toward the chasm beneath, and exhaling stress. The man watched on through the glass; his eyes were hungry for a taste of her. Tonight, she decided to ignore routine. She lifted herself out of the bath. The water followed the curves of her body before they drained away. The luscious red towel absorbed the remnants on her skin. She moved toward the window holding her finger an inch away from the glass. His finger followed her to the front door. She could see the hazy outline of his figure through the translucent glass panel. The system clicked as access was granted to enter. Turning her back on him, she led the way to her studio before locking the door behind her. The room was soundproofed, she liked to work in silence. He joined her on a large white canvas that was spread across the floor. After removing his clothes, she took his rough hands in hers and coated them in raspberry macaroon paint. His hands began to wander across her body. She coated her palms in satin black and clawed at his back. Bringing him with her, they sank to the floor. Their two bodies operated as one until she plunged her hands into the paint can, ecstasy. Her husband sipped his champagne in the next room.

There was leftover pancake mixture in the fridge the next morning. She poured the batter into the stainless steel pan, pretending it had been freshly made, and waited. Her husband took his seat at the table, sipped his freshly squeezed orange juice, and waited for his breakfast. The pancakes were stacked three high, drizzled with lemon juice, sprinkled with rose petals and decorated with hibiscus flowers. She served him the handmade ceramic plate, glazed azure topped with her creation. The canvas from the previous night, a mixture of mud, leaves, paint and bodily fluids hung over the fireplace behind her husband. She returned to the kitchen counter to make herself breakfast but lost herself in the vast sea in front of her. The red sun was still rising, a haze on the cold morning; its colour saturated the landscape. She peeled away at the flesh of an orange before sinking her teeth into it. Juice squirted onto the table, creating a distinctive pattern on the marble in front of her: the height of an orgasm or the scene of a crime left on the clean surface. She wiped the surface clean and returned to her husband who was waiting for his goodbye kiss.

She followed as he left the house and watched as he put his leather suitcase in the boot of the car. Her favourite part of the day was watching him leave. Once he had disappeared into the distance, she wandered toward her studio. Her black silk dressing gown was embroidered with small pink flowers which grew off a tree on her back. It flowed when she walked as though there was a soft breeze causing the tree to sway. Her dressing gown slipped down her shoulder as she laid another white canvas on the floor, hoping this would be her masterpiece. The man from the previous night stood in the window. She sat down in front of her easel and spread her legs. His emerald eyes locked on her body as she opened the dressing gown. She had his attention.

The Lamborghini had paused on its journey. His black OnePlus had been left on the sleek oak side table by the door. Fortunately, he had not driven far before realising it was not in the car. To quell nerves before a presentation, he would listen to a recording of his script which was saved on his phone. He found a small road to turn around and drove back to the house. The car rolled into the driveway. He slipped his phone into the red silk pocket of his suit jacket and walked toward his wife's studio. White paper lined the floor like snowfall across the Fens. He opened his arms to embrace his wife when a naked man entered the room. He pushed his wife behind him, to protect her: the safety system had been compromised. His right fist connected with the naked stranger's face, knocking him onto the canvas. His wife locked the door. Sitting on his chest, he began pounding at this man's petrified face with his fist. Blood sprayed onto the canvas igniting the fire in her eyes. Her heart pounded in her chest. The man had stopped breathing. Seizing the knife from the table, she repeatedly punched the blade into her husband's back. This would be her masterpiece. Blood scattered itself across the blank page like red confetti at a wedding. She grinned. There was no life left in her husband's body. Pushing him aside, she straddled the naked man, pushing his chin backward until the skin was taught. With the blade clutched in her fist, she severed his throat. Blood poured, like a waterfall of viscous red paint, down his neck and onto the canvas. She dipped her hands into the satin black paint and pushed them through the blood as if she were swimming through the Styx. The bodies were discarded to either side. Her body was coated in blood as she stood up and admired her work. Her painting was complete. This would be her greatest creation. Picking up the phone with her bloodied hand, she dialled her husband's work number:

I'm sorry, Daniel cannot make the presentation today.

EMBRACING
Elizabeth Yew

The mountain strangles and roots me still; the wind whips and wraps its fingers around my body, forcing me to turn
   to the direction of the land I once called Home. The choking embrace I tore away from, its addictive hollowness which chased. The grim
   silhouette of perpetual darkness tightening its grasp on me, draped over my limping body like a chilling blanket, as I struggle to crawl—

   pathetically away. From
Home,
        who traps ants in transparent lunchboxes and shakes, laughing as they skitter through the labyrinth of concrete and cars and soulless people;
   who looks so striking in a dress of burning sunset, wounding those who touch the sharpened peaks of Victoria, as the cascade of sunlight immortalises in small black cages;
   whose skyline glows with artificial clouds as people murmur glints of recognition but never certain enough to utter our names out loud;
   who when searched, sees the intertwined domes of egg puffs, buns of dim sum steaming in hot bamboo crates, and dark slabs of Argyle Street and Nathan Road-
   who hides herself behind the curtain of the inventor, drowning in Money soaked in Red;
   revealing her bone-deep scars only to those who choose to stay behind, to cherish the ugliness of her. only then does she unlock the cell

   which holds the shamefulness of
Reality.
who shudders in despair from having its grand streets of neon signs and domino billboards littered with screaming profanities and flying concrete stones.
   who was smeared in splattered blood with faceless, bodiless fingers who hide behind walls of the law and plastic black shields of injustice. Their oppression
   forced our mothers to kneel and beg, cries of fury and fear silenced by a shot in the skull.
   who pulled at her neck as toxic gases invade her lungs, main street turned warfront and into dark alleyways with armed silhouettes cornering innocent victims, batons at the ready.

   who
I,
      Abandoned and left.
      when the paint of my hair and inks in my skin offended Home because I was a bursting array of colour in a black-and-white city.

I abandoned and left,
> when who I kiss and dance with can lead to a life behind a black barred cage.

I abandoned and left,
> when Home lied about progress. Made to muffle my silence.

I abandoned and left,
> when her streets are deafening with judgemental snares and unfiltered glares as we reach for each other.

I abandoned and left,
when Home taught me to be shameful of who I am.

I abandoned and left,
> when Home whispered into the ears of my parents: Stop loving this broken and incomplete creature.

I abandoned and left,
> when I knew confessing would be futile.

I abandoned and left,
> when Home told me she no longer has love left for me.

NEW ADDRESS BOOK
Ella Pamment

Welcome to your 'NEW ADDRESS BOOK'! Unlike other address books, here you can document who you meet, in the correct order you meet them, helping you to establish lasting relationships! So, get stuck in! Congratulations on your NEW home!

MOVED IN: 16th March 2015
ADDRESS: 20 Whyville Close, Lightville, M1S SNG

FIRST IMPRESSIONS of your home village are SO important! That's why we have given you the opportunity to record how you're settling in. In regular intervals—every month—you will be able to record how you are progressing!

CHECK IN 1—Moving into a quaint village, I wanted to get away from the politics of a city. A quiet life and meeting interesting people with a story to tell is my goal—normal people! Yes, normal people who don't talk at you about the economics of the city. A quiet life is what I'm here for.

NAME: Neighbour Left
ADDRESS: 19 Whyville Close, Lightville, BUB BLY
NOTE: Very hyperactive woman. Seems to have a lot going on—she runs sixteen clubs in the weekdays alone, gets up each day for Pilates and hosts a jumble sale in the village hall every other Saturday. She has four children. I am invited for dinner every Thursday night. Don't ask her if she has pets—her cat got run over yesterday.

NAME: Neighbour Right. ~~Brian. Ryan?~~ Bobby.
ADDRESS: 21 Whyville Close, Lightville, CR3 3PY
NOTE: I think his name is Brian? Ryan? Bobby? Doesn't blink when he talks to you. Spits when he speaks and insists on hugging you before you talk and after talking—always ten seconds, and always ten seconds too long. Would not leave a dead mouse in his care. AVOID.

NAME: Church Lady with her blind dog
ADDRESS: 1 Whyville close, Lightville, STR NGE
NOTE: Scared of her own shadow. Her dog shakes less than her and it's blind. Quiet talker. Doesn't like the coffee at church: too watery. Her head bops as she speaks to you. Has a stare and absent smile that quite literally penetrates your soul. She will not leave you alone for hours on end and when she does, she tells you to 'take care' with an ominous continuous nod of her missing mind. I am petrified that her nervous nod will give her whiplash.

NAME: Rector
ADDRESS: White Chapel House, Whyville Close, Lightville, B0R EDD
NOTE: Jovial man when not preaching—when he is, he is in slow motion. If the old people weren't wishing to die yet, they certainly are now. Looks as if he has the weight of the world on his shoulders—Jesus does not seem to be on his side —which does not bode well for his sermon of 'The Lord is with you always' where the old man who had just awoken half way through wrongly stated 'and also with you'. The thirty minute service that took one hour and a half has certainly made you reconsider atheism as an avenue.

NAME: Church Woman in chair
ADDRESS: No idea, had to document
NOTE: Feeling awful now, at the time all I could hear was a whoosh sound every two seconds from the woman sat in the pew in front of me. I became increasingly irritated. I considered asking her to move forward. It took me far too long to realise it was an oxygen machine! Lord forgive me.

NAME: Tambourine Tantrum.
ADDRESS: 13 Whyville Close, Lightville, MAD NES
NOTE: Rattled a tambourine at the back of the church service. Coiled ribbons during hymns. Sang as if it was an opera. Realised afterwards that she is not only VERY enthusiastic in the church, but also in the yoga community. She told me if I ever wanted to meet for a recreational camping trip in the woods to delve closer to the Lord, I would be more than welcome. She went back to dancing with ribbons. Revoking faith.

CHECK IN 2—What a whirlwind. There has been an array of people I have met. What can I say? What a lively bunch, such enthusiastic people ready to greet you! I wasn't expecting such a warm welcome. Warm as in likening them to wetting yourself—stuck to you, and uncomfortable. Where the hell have I moved to?

NAME: Samantha
ADDRESS: 14 Whyville Close, Lightville, MUR D3R
NOTE: Likes coffee, hates gardening, drinks wine at weekends and in the mornings, and has a stable job—lovely woman. ~~I think I shall become friends with her!~~ She ran over my neighbour's cat. Fuck.

NAME: Basically Vicky Pollard (Do not call her Vicky… this is not her real name)
ADDRESS: 11 Whyville Close, Lightville, CH4 VVY
NOTE: Neon pink tracksuit with 'STACE' written in diamantes on her back. T's in words are a sound of the past or on holiday in a multiverse. Walks as if she has stubbed her toe, and has two children. Will tell you how her brother's girlfriend's cousin's mum's uncle's grandad's friend's daughter's husband was the man to invent the toaster. Spoiler—he was not. She will then tell you how she used to be

'cool' when she would sit in the park with her boyfriend, who has now left her for her cousin. Entertaining to say the least. AVOID.

NAME: ~~Gobby Gina~~ Gina
ADDRESS: 9 Whyville Close, Lightville, CH4 TTY
NOTE: Gina proceeded to tell me how the mains pipe burst last Thursday and how that has indeed contributed to the taxes of the economy—it hasn't. Then told me how her cousin gave birth and has hemorrhoids, but she can't repeat this and that her brother got herpes. Gina's mother is in hospital as she fell backwards onto a bath tap—an awkward call to the paramedics I am sure—and that her father left her mother because she is an alcoholic, and Kerry down the road is only short and fat because she has a thyroid issue. AVOID.

NAME: Olly
ADDRESS: 8 Whyville Close, Lightville, VRY OLD
NOTE: A man that looks deceased having a pint in the pub. He looks like he crawled out of the church yard. Most likely resurrected by the fear in the soul of the blind lady's dog who basically shivers and cries 24/7. He looks like the human embodiment of a prune. He told me in a deep hoarse voice that this pub was built in 1456 originally. He has been sat in this chair since that date. Sweet old man, probably only three more days on top of his three centuries already gone left to live.

NAME: Alison
ADDRESS: 6 Whyville Close, Lightville, STR ESD
NOTE: Seen her out of the village speeding. I asked her about it during her village speed watch presentation and—I quote—she said, "I speed but not in Lightville, it's not the same!". Wit of a comedian, common sense of a dead bat. Seen her driving out of our village—shouting at cyclists calling them "suicide on wheels". Would go and meet her for wine again soon.

CHECK IN 3—Where do I start? The city is diverse, but this is something else. I'm unsure if I've lost brain_cells, or if I am merely unfazed now by the most obscure people. WHAT IS GOING ON?!?

NAME: Baggy Brenda
ADDRESS: 4 Whyville Close, Lightville, BAG GED
NOTE: An old woman. Looks like ET. Hunched over from carrying her body weight in bags. You may see her and wonder what the hell is in her bags. She is carrying roughly six bags full of bags and nothing else—no fruit, no shopping, no water, no medicine. Bags. She will not allow you to also carry her bags full of bags. That would evidently be against the bag laws of the bag world that she is bagging within. I do not understand her. She will not speak to you. She will not look at you. She will continue to walk with her baggage down the road until

she gets to the bottom, puts her bags down, and then turns around, picks them up and goes around again. What in the world of bags is going on with her? She does this daily.

NAME: ~~Lady with no life other than to complain.~~ Rosemary
ADDRESS: 6 Whyville Close, Lightville, M0A NER
NOTE: If you're feeling down, Rosemary will quite simply finish you off. She decided to tell me how my neighbour on the left wanted to apply for planning permission. She said no. She asked the farmer to say no. He said no. He asked his wife on the Parish Council to say no. She said no and then no planning was achieved. Apparently, the village has never been so over-crowded with people who didn't belong here. Has a set of mushroom statues in the garden—which look like a wooden phallic museum. She seems unaware of this.

NAME: Babysitter
ADDRESS: 3 Whyville Close, Lightville, B1T CCH
NOTE: Works as a part time babysitter. Witnessed an ordeal—a woman with wet hair shouted at her on her driveway because of something she had done towards her daughter. Quite the commotion. She will not be hired.

NAME: ~~Wet hair woman~~ Village footcare
ADDRESS: 2 Whyville Close, Lightville, IC0 NIC
NOTE: Looks after the elderly. Feisty. Spoke to her in passing. Says the people who are passive in the village are "more laid back than people in a morgue". Despises people who have, as she would say, "the IQ of a toaster… a broken toaster". Would hire her for an evening for entertainment purposes if nothing else.

CHECK IN 4—Speechless. I live among these people. All my moral fibers are disintegrating. I have lost faith in humankind. What on earth is even going on? Who even am I? Who even are these people? Get me out of here.

NAME: Estate Agents
ADDRESS: 46 Lincoln Drive, Lightville, G3T 0UT
NOTE: Open 9-5 every Tuesday, Wednesday, and Sunday. Does everyone do everything in a backwards, front to diagonal direction in this place?!?

NAME: Refurbishment men
ADDRESS: 87 Hupper Drive, Lightville, STU P1D
NOTE: One might kill you, the other might not notice for a week. One said that his girlfriend had started making him exotic foods—she fed him an onion. He said he likes to tie dye—for context this wasn't a conversation with him, but he went on about his hobby and the struggle of dyes for fifteen minutes rather than working. AVOID.

NAME: Removal men
ADDRESS: Range House, 7 River Close, Hapville, N0R MAL
NOTE: Moving date: 16th of July

NAME:
ADDRESS:
NOTE:

NAME:
ADDRESS:
NOTE:

NAME:
ADDRESS:
NOTE:

THE HUM
Ellen Newall

I was born with a tiny hole in my heart. My mom told me when I was six that my EKGs were measuring all of the electricity in my body. I got a static shock from the nylon sheets rubbing against the metal bed and imagined sparks shooting into my heart under the sticky circles.

Now, strobing sparks were firing, making my whole body vibrate in frozen agony. I could still hear humming through the mechanical crackling and hot splatters of light. And then, all was black. The crackling was gone, but the humming penetrated its way through the emptiness. All I could smell was burnt coffee.

I never liked Dunkin Donuts' coffee. I used to go to the Dunkins outside my work twice a day; once in the morning and once in the evening. The shop always smelt dirty. The smell of stale beans mixed with chocolate syrup made me cough. One really cold morning, the week before, when I was out with Seb. He made a joke about seeing mum at work going in for chemo with the label still stuck to her wig. When I stumbled into Dunkins the next day before work, I was still 30% alcohol and 100% fragile, and I burst into tears when the girl told me to have a nice day.

I smiled vaguely at her when I reached the counter. The man in front was taking forever and the smell of cigarettes wafted off his jacket. I had been feeling fuzzy for the past few days, but today it seemed worse. There was a dull humming noise constantly in the background. I grimaced, irritated at my headphones. I slipped them out, but somehow the grumbling was still there. I turned around to see if there was a motorcycle or car leaving its engine idle, but the parking lot was empty apart from my car. I always checked my car.

"Ma'am?"

The guy in front was finally done. I asked if the speaker was busted.

"We don't have a speaker ma'am."

It got louder. I bought an americano. When she turned around I hastily dug my finger deep into my ear to loosen any wax. But as I pulled it out, it was somehow louder. The girl had turned back around to me. I could see her mouth moving, but I could only hear humming. My back broke out into a cold sweat and I began to tremble as the sound wrapped around me. Her eyebrows cocked, concerned and her mouth made the shape of: Ma'am? Are you ok?

I deafly shoved my fist into my purse, threw a ten-dollar note onto the counter and ran home, leaving my car in the parking lot.

I awoke a few hours later to a concerned shake of my shoulder. Seb was standing over me, confused.

"You ok?"

I couldn't hear it anymore. Seb nodded as I explained and said with a tap of his ear: "You're hearing things."

I looked at him.

"See an ENT if it comes back. Gotta bounce. I've been asked to help with a hysterectomy."

His round cheeks lifted in a grin as he turned the light off. He kissed my forehead and left.

I lay awake in the dark until my eyes grew too heavy to stay open. I woke up with a start to hear my roommate Martha come home hours later. The humming had returned.

From then onwards, that terrible hum never left me and I was left to seek a solution. I took onboard Seb's suggestion of seeing an ENT. I sat staunchly in the waiting room. Waiting for that damned ball of wax to be yanked from my cavities so I could experience delicious relief. But that relief was not to come.

"You're all clear," Doctor WhatsHisName said, "you must be hearing things."

I felt dejected. I had been unable to sleep every night that fortnight. Either, I had been thinking over that dastardly hum, or it had been keeping me awake. I tried to find other ENTs, begging for help with my problem. Eventually, they stopped returning my calls. I became more desperate. Within a matter of a month, the hum had consumed me, echoing through my skull with its mocking vibrato.

I lay in bed every night half-conscious after I had checked to see if the window was closed. After I had turned off every source of electricity. But the humming always found a way in. It leaked through the cracks in the floors and walls. Every drop sent sparks through my head, the low frequency causing my spine to tremble. I was mummified as it sunk into every pore, every hole.

"Thea?"

It had been three months now. I was sitting hunched on the floor like a frog, eyeing the pieces of paper plastered neatly on the wall. As I turned around, I felt my vertebrae grind. Seb was leaning on the door frame, annoyed.

"It's 3 AM."

I turned back around to face the wall and rested my chin on my knees. I wished I had more information.

"You coming to bed?"

I heard him walk up behind me. I could see his stout shadow grow bigger on the wall.

"You really went ham on Martha's room when she moved out."

He reached over and stroked the first article I had pinned on there.

I remember coming home from the third ENT three months ago when I had spotted the headline in a kiosk. I dove across the street and gripped it so hard that I thought my knuckles might rip.

The Hum: the sound driving 2% of the population crazy

My legs pounded on the concrete, though not quite outrunning the hum. I burst headfirst through the front door and caught a sliver of my reflection in the den mirror. My eyes were swollen with fat bags and my hair was limp. Even the mole on my upper lip was trembling. I needed a wall. Not my bedroom, the sticky tack would stain. I didn't think twice before heading towards Martha's bedroom. She was hardly there. I only ever saw her when she came to collect clothes to stay at her boyfriend's house. She had no use for walls. A few hours later, Martha arrived for those clothes. She had a different opinion when she saw the hot-from-the-printer paper enveloping her walls. Many expletives interrupting my explanations later, Martha had vanished with a final slam of the front door. I drifted to the sound of the hum to Martha's empty bed with hot tears staining my cheeks. I stared at the papers on the wall, the newspaper clipping nestled in the centre.

The collection grew over the next few months. It felt like second nature wandering to the spare bedroom with my arms full of paper. The guts of my project lined the wall with red strings going from sheet to sheet. Seb called my house unhinged. The rooms echoed and severed wires carpeted the floor. Plastered holes cloaked the walls and ceiling. He didn't enjoy spending time here.

I asked Seb if the TV was off every night at his place. He was nothing but a ghost to me. He slinked past me to bed after a mandatory kiss on the forehead. I was sat on the edge of the bed. I turned to look at his body under the covers. He wasn't even looking at me now.

"It's off."

I told him he was lying. Without saying anything, Seb reached for the remote and clicked the *on* switch, but the TV stayed black.

"Get over it, Thea."

I stood up and went to the outlet. It was unplugged. Seb's eyes were staring but he wouldn't see me. I got back into bed with my back to him, staring at the therapist's number he had taped to my phone.

The next Tuesday when Seb came home, my arm was through his wall and a handful of wires hung like limp spaghetti in my fist. I could see the vein that throbbed on his forehead when he was angry. We stared at each other in semi humming silence that was thick, but not honeyed. Cutting the wires hadn't worked. He didn't raise his voice. I needed screaming to drown it out.

"Just because your mom is sick, doesn't mean you have to be. Get a therapist."

Those were the last words he said to me. The door shut with a muffled slam and I was left gripping my crumpled notes. I took the top sheet and smoothed the furrowed wrinkles out against the closed door of his apartment:

Parish Street
Fourth tower

I stopped going to work after that. I never found out if I got fired. Doctors had stopped picking up my calls long ago. I received an email last week:

Ms Thea Huang,

We hope this email finds you well. We are contacting you to make you aware that due to your overuse of our system, we have made the decision to pass your details to the Detroit Psychiatric Institute. They shall be contacting you shortly.

Sincerely,
DMC Family Health Centre

I cut off my power for good that evening, partially to avoid the DPI's threat. I sat by the light of stiff candles that were bubbling over with pellets of melted wax. I couldn't hear their spits through the plugs buried in my ears. I squinted over my progress on the wall. Big, red sharpie crosses marked my failures. The fourth pylon connected to the small power grid on Parish Street was my next target. It chortled at me when I used to drive to the office with electric splutters.

I had cut many wires in my apparent lunacy. I had snipped the odd neighbour's power off. The slender pads of my fingers were worn smooth long ago. I had never, however, committed the crime of trespassing.

The bolt cutters felt foreign in my hands when they cracked the chain at the grid. The building was not big, but in the dark of 5:14 AM, the metal walls echoed with enormous stillness.

It didn't take me long to find the power grid itself. The skin on my neck crawled as my fingers pried open the closed door. I approached with caution, desperate to find the right switch, the right cable to slice. But I was met with a spaghetti junction of wires. The humming began to grow louder and my heart began to shake. My hand hovered this way and that. Every graze over the wires felt like needles running up my fingers to my eardrums.

God, I just wanted it to be over. How could I have been so foolish to believe it would be so simple?

I felt a rough hand on my shoulder. I had stupidly worn my earplugs. With a choked yelp, I was pulled around to see a man. He was short with a thick neck and a mop clutched in his thicker hand.

"How did you get in here?"

Without waiting for me to reply, he removed his hand from my shoulder and pulled a phone out of his pocket.

My eyes widened and I began to beg him. I spluttered out my story, screaming to him that if I just cut that wire I could be free. If he could have the heart to give me mercy.

When his thick finger hit the dial button, my anxiety transitioned to pure panic.

I looked down and the bolt cutter had suddenly collided with the man's head.

He was now lying spreadeagled with blood blooming on his temple.

I could see now how young he was. He was not a man, just a boy.

Through the raging hum, I could hear a concerned mumble from the phone on the floor. I lunged and grabbed the wires to rip the life out of them.

And then it got so much louder.

SEASALT FOOTSTEPS
Emma Mcdonald

Walking Forward
He stepped out of reach of lapping, stone-skipped waves,
rings of salt crusted around his ankles,
small sunlight handprints baked against his skin,
his head hung as he walked away.

Rings of salt crusted around his ankles,
memories of sand trailed behind on the concrete,
his head hung as he walked away,
the only trace of him specs of sand.

Memories of sand trailed behind on the concrete,
they caught the diluted pink of the sunset,
the only trace of him specs of sand,
lingered like a child's glitter long after their echoes of laughter faded grey.

They caught the diluted pink of the sunset
small sunlight handprints baked against his skin
lingered like a child's glitter long after their echoes of laughter faded grey.
He stepped out of reach of lapping, stone-skipped waves, holding

Talisman
child's castle bucket
sun-bleached and side cracked like the
fossilised imprint
of a wishbone carried by
a sobbing father's chilled hands.

Sunset
He carried his daughter, the warmth of a small hand in his now unencumbered;
no-one says how much remembrance weighs.
He watched his footprints and wondered

how long until both he and his daughter are unremembered?
Grief borne alone is forgetting, painfully delayed
as the darkness drowns them despite the sunbird.

Retreating Tide
Bucket placed on the
seat, sigh, moved to the footwell.
No need for child lock.
Seasalt replaced by stale air,
home, head on the wheel, tears thawed.

Cliffside Baptism
Smart suit of soft, egg-shell blue hung heavy on his shoulders,
the limestone swallowed the echo of his steps
between pews spaced like skipping stones,
conversations bubbled around him.

The limestone swallowed the echo of his steps,
palms cupped over a candle flame, eyes closed, frost fell away from his bones,
conversations bubbled around him,
the priest stood at the front of the hall among a shoal of family.

Palms cupped over a candle flame, eyes closed, frost fell away from his bones,
his niece met his eyes and walked to him with her crying baby,
the priest stood at the front of the hall among a shoal of family,
she handed him the baby, who cried harder - he laughed; rocked like a boat at harbour.

His niece met his eyes and walked to him with her crying baby
between pews spaced like skipping stones
she handed him the baby, who cried harder—he laughed; rocked like a boat at harbour,
soft, egg-shell blue cushioned her head as they watched the sun glitter on the waves together.

Sea-breeze Prayer
Glitter sunlight waves,
eyesight dazzled, memories
caught on sea salt winds,
salt in his throat choking sobs
finally dried, sun-warmed skin.

Lost at Sea
She never understood why she couldn't make snow-angels in sand,
it would shift under her and she'd roll, giggling, into the sea,
he always had to wade into the waves to rescue her headband.

She settled for seashell-studded castles that needed his help to stand,
calling, *Daddy, dig the moat deeper!* until she could wade in it, smile wide with glee.
She never understood why she couldn't make snow-angels in sand.

She would doodle secret letters on the beach by hand,
drum her bucket in time with the waves, then in the car with sand-cuffed dungarees.
He always had to wade into the waves before they left, to rescue her headband.

She hadn't cried at her baptism, but screwed up her face like a displeased clam
so he took her to swim; mermaids, dolphins and whales imagined swimming free.
She never understood why she couldn't make snow-angels in sand.

He considered writing to her on the beach, but could only stand
watching the tide wash away any play-tanned memory
of how she never understood why she couldn't make snow-angels in sand.
He waded into the waves and held her headband, tight in his hands.

Oyster
Couldn't hold his girl,
glitter sun or candle flame
held this baby close.

JUST IN CASE
Ersi Zevgoli

She is running late. As always.

She should've made it to the flat by twelve, it's pushing on twenty past. By the time Anna turns into Chapelfield Gardens, the drizzle that started as she left the police station is a full on storm. Her raincoat hood stops being effective, and begins to let the drops seep through.

Head bent down, she almost misses the man.

Almost.

She looks up, and there, in the empty park, he sits. Alone. She can't tell much about him. He's holding up an umbrella that obscures his face from her gaze. The only thing visible is a book cover: *How To Disappear.*

Anna doesn't have time to stop and examine, take a closer look, even as her curiosity - her detective sense, as her son used to call it when he was little and still impressionable - rises like the wind picking up. Rain hits her face, making her blink. With a last look at the man, Anna lowers her head once more and walks briskly on.

Who would brave this rain to sit outside in January and read? Someone who has no choice. Or at least feels that he has no choice. Something about his posture, his leaning back with one leg lazily draped over the other, something about the dated jeans and the brown, tattered trainers tells her that he is a middle-aged man, a man past youth and vitality.

Someone who is desperate to disappear, disintegrate, dissipate into the particles of air that surround him. Anna feels a peculiar sort of kinship with the man. As she exits the park, she dares a glance towards his bench. It is hard to make him out - he has blended into the rain, the trees, the grey January air thick with something indescribable that crushes the soul. It takes her a moment to make him out, just, over there. Her lips twitch: that book must contain some solid advice.

She's almost there. Winchester Tower. She switches her detective sense off - what her son would beg her to do as soon as she walked through the door every night, late.

It's a procedural thing, police are required to be there when a council flat is broken into by the housing people. Just in case. In case… Of what?

The tower rises above her in the grey sky, as bleak as its backdrop. She checks Forrest's text: Mary C. Waters, flat 12. She starts climbing the stairs, glad, oh so glad, to have something more substantial than her useless raincoat covering her head.

She knows she's in the right place before she reaches it. Jason Forrest paces in front of the door, each step more menacing than the last. Or at least that's what he thinks. He looks wet, annoyed, and ridiculous. He sighs. It is a weird mixture of annoyance, impatience, relief. It is a sigh that would've sped Anna up when she was younger, when she cared what people thought of her.

"Took your sweet time," he tells her as he stubs out a cigarette butt with the heel of his boot.

"Hello to you too." If looks could kill, they say. If they could wither you to your core. If they could make the sky greyer. "Come on, let's get this over with," says Anna, taking her badge out.

Forrest gives a nod towards the door to the two uniforms. They bash the door in, no issue. There is hardly any resistance from the insubstantial lock and weathered hinges. Silence. No, not silence exactly. The heavy rain hitting the walls all around, the unintelligible sound of distant conversation heard through the now open door is not silence. Anna looks at Forrest. He is staring back at her, mirroring the expression she must be making.

"Police! Don't move!" Anna shouts, hand brandishing her badge in front of her like an ineffective shield.

Nothing. The conversation goes on, unfazed, uninterrupted. Music washes over it, obscuring it, blurring it.

"Police!" Forrest shouts, just in case Anna's female voice isn't enough of a threat. Just in case. In years gone by, her eye would've twitched in sheer annoyance.

Anna's cheeks are frozen - no, hold on. No. They are scalding hot. She feels the veins beneath her skin dilating from the sudden change of cold to extreme heat. She notices it exiting the flat in a staggering wave. It's as if a portal has opened, from a freezing January afternoon in Norwich, to a summer midday on a Greek island. The music turns again, and it's the BBC News theme. Even diluted as it is in the freezing air, the heat emanating from the open door is stifling. And what is that smell? Sickly sweet, like pungent decay, and—

Oh no. Oh please God, no.

Anna's hand drops to her side as she walks into the flat. She doesn't bother taking cover or calling for reinforcement. She doesn't keep quiet, she takes no precautions. All that training, all that experience, all that protocol is left at the doorstep, excess baggage that can only weigh her down. The protocol is useless in this case. The case of the just in case. She is living the exception.

She hears Forrest's voice whispering "Dunne, what the fuck are you doing?" but it barely registers. She is consumed by the heat and the smell and the news being read aloud. She makes her way down the hallway, past the tiny little kitchen, and into the tiny little lounge, where the telly is playing on and on and on and on for who knows how long, and the radiator has been keeping the flat abnormally warm. The smell is so overpowering here that she feels her scant breakfast and numerous coffees churning close to her esophagus, flirting with her throat, mouth, with the open air.

The lights are on. The string lights on the small, dusty Christmas tree blink, most of them burnt out. Wrapped presents are stacked underneath, and in front of those—

Anna doubles over and throws up on her own feet. The bitter aftertaste of bile stays in her mouth, as she straightens herself. She looks again at the skeletal hands clutching an Aldi shopping bag, whatever was once inside it long turned into mush along with the person holding it. Empty eye sockets, bones peeking out of rotten flesh and decaying clothes, greying hair still intact atop the skull that's covered in gunk and maggots and—

She feels pure bile rise up inside her.

"Forrest", she calls through the open door. "Call Forensics and the Coroner's office." Over the newsreader, she hears his heavy footfalls in the hallway. "*Don't come in here.*"

He ignores her. The two uniforms come in as well, but Anna turns and walks towards the kitchen. She hears their disgusted grunts, their exclamations to whatever gods may be, their rushing back outside to the sanctuary of the rain and fresh air. She starts opening cupboards, the fridge, looking through the dusty papers, searching for receipts, best before dates, anything.

The contents of the fridge have turned to slush almost as horrifying as the remains in the lounge. Everything is dated from before November 2017. Even the tins of soup in the cupboard have expired.

Two years. Anna takes measured steps towards the entrance. She can hear the uniforms on the phone to the police station, the coroner, moving the process along. She leans against the railing next to Forrest.

No one noticed. How could no one notice? Mary C. Waters, how did you slip away unnoticed? All those presents, they were meant for someone. You wrapped them up yourself, a full month ahead of time. You were looking forward to seeing them, spending time with them, reading stupid Christmas jokes out of crackers, and wearing the little paper crowns. And then - what? You just disappeared. Did no one look for you? Did no one notice? Did no one care?

Anna breathes in the cold air, glad of its bite, glad that she can feel it on her cheeks and isn't lying dead in her own decaying skin. She finds her mind turning to the man in the park. She wonders, eager as he was to escape, to disappear, to be left alone, would he change his mind looking at Mary C. Waters' body? Would he be filled with the same dread that she feels restricting her throat, or would he gaze at the forgotten woman with morbid admiration? To disappear, to truly disappear, to be left alone, you have to be dead for a year in your miserable little council flat, without anyone having bothered to check on you, worry about you, file a missing persons report on you. Is that what you are after, then?

The overwhelming awareness that she hasn't spoken to her son in a week snaps Anna out of that train of thought. She looks down at her silent phone in her hand. Not a call, not a text, nothing. She's been working too hard, coming home too late, being too tired and too preoccupied, only just managing to keep it together. As always.

"You all right, Dunne?"

Forrest's voice is gentler than she's ever heard it. She looks at him, his forehead creased, his face ashen, his self-importance nowhere to be seen.

"Yeah, yeah, I just… Shock. I'll be fine."

Anna reverts to Detective Inspector Dunne, and it's not till early evening that Forensics are done with the scene. The remains of Mary C. Waters are taken to the mortuary, but the Coroner suspects natural causes. It will be difficult, impossible, to determine at this stage of decomposition. An inquest will be opened, but who will care about the death of an old lady who lived alone, who no one bothered checking in on for a whole year?

Walking back to the police station, Anna makes sure to cross through Chapelfield Gardens again. Disregarding the wet darkness that surrounds her, she walks past the bench she saw the man sitting on. It is empty. She releases a breath she is not aware she is holding, and a strange brand of relief fills her. The relief of projecting her own fears and troubles onto an unknown man in the park. He disappeared from her—she hopes he hasn't yet disappeared to those who matter to him.

It's past nine when she turns the key to her flat. Anna drops her bag by the door, walks into the kitchen, and without taking off her soaked raincoat, sits at the table. She pulls out her phone, and after a few failed attempts—her fingers are not cooperating, frozen and damp as they are - manages to unlock it. She dials a number she knows by heart, and brings the phone to her ear. It rings. And it rings. And it rings. Before the fourth ring, she hears her son's chirpy, if tired, voice.

"Hi, mum, how's it going?"

STARS AND STRIPES
Esther Jardine

They carry whole sections of their world
In small fabric squares,
Whole groups represented by colours and markings
Caught in their proud, divisive snares.

The fabric is as weak as their unity
Which turns to hate for those not under their own sign-
Symbols of fear and obedience
Laying claim to land, their moon, planets like mine.

Yet, as their history shows,
Symbols can create belonging,
Communities who support without oppressing others.
It is the story which gives them meaning.

I have learned to read their symbols as well as words,
They speak of families, traditions, and homes,
The colours of pride, of both power and resistance,
Diverse signs, all meaning 'unique, but not alone'.

Although it is only too human
To attach such weight to cloth and colours,
Occasionally, I dream my home has its own flag,
As I search for it among the endless stars.

THE SAME HANDS
Eve Colabella

I am pinching myself in circles,
clots of bitter plum juice staining
the surface of my skin like numbers
bruised onto an alarm clock: wake up
wake up wake up

An ongoing fever-dream of heavy
bass and unwanted hands, and you
flashing in the corners of my peripheral
(*always flashing*), stumbling with vacant
eyes onto the ground, I look down on you

and do not know who you are anymore.

A handprint on white, unremovable,
and I can never wear that halter-neck
again, how can your sober touch be
so gentle and wary?—you who
can guide me across a charging
force of traffic and somehow stop
the danger from reaching us—

I do not know who you are anymore.

I am trying to extract pieces of you
from the rubble, separate the twinkle
of Christmas lights from the blinding
flash of strobe, my arms feel tired from
missing the beforehand. I know I should
not be trying to divide the lights, instead

I should glue them together in one, messy
monoprint of a boy I thought I knew—but I
remember your hands trembling when I told
you what you had done, the same, soft hands
whose slippery palms have stained every round
part of my memory;

they cannot be the same hands.

I do not know who you are anymore.

I wish that it was blotted out for me
as it was for you, that all I had left
were words recounted in shivering
soliloquy, not the feeling of fingers
crawling down my back, moments
of silence being deafened by the distant
thump of that song that was screaming
as you untied the knot that we had been
tightening and watched the rope fall limply
to the sticky, beer-coated floor with my
polaroid of you.

An imposter has crept into my rose-coloured
waters and I am trying so hard to detect him
in the pictures of us, that even today, I cannot
stop rifling through.

I do not know who you are anymore.

MAGNAPINNA
Fin Doktor

We've been coming to this beach every summer for as long as I can remember so it ain't like me being down here on my own means I'm hiding from no one. If I was hiding, I would've picked someplace only I knew and besides, I'll head back up to the cottage soon enough, so no one's got no reason to say I ain't acting friendly to Lottie or Mr and Mrs Westby. The three of them visit us here every year. Used to be there were four of them, but their son, who's Noah's age, don't come with them no more. Him and Noah never really got on like me and Lottie get on, even after Mum asked him to try and act more friendly. Noah's real smart but he ain't always good with people and sometimes I think it makes him get lonely, like how even though he's three years older than us he still takes to following me and Lottie around whenever we go rockpooling, hanging back a little, acting like he ain't listening to what we're saying, or like he's reading his book even though his eyes ain't moving, all the while waiting for something to come up that only he'd know the answer to so he can jump in and show his smarts. Like last year when we was down at the rockpools and Lottie and me were looking for lobsters but all we could find was crabs and Noah was sitting nearby with his book, and we was wondering how come we never find no orange crabs like what there is on telly or like gets washed up and Noah said without looking up that, well, it were the heat what actually turns their shells orange and we was getting confused with having seen crabs what had been cooked.

But what about them shells that wash up? I asked him. *They ain't been cooked.*

That'd be the sun, I'd imagine, he said, jerking his head upwards and I shielded my eyes and looked up too then turned back to Lottie who was squatting beside me prodding at a limpet with a stick all quiet like she gets whenever Noah's talking.

Well, what about that? I said. *No wonder we can't find none.*

Lottie just scowled. *I think that's dreadful what with showing them as orange on telly if it ain't like that in real life. They ought to be ashamed of themselves, making people look soft for not knowing.*

Noah's real smart like I say and I were always asking him to explain this thing or that thing to me what I'd seen in one of his books he'd left open. There were this one time when he was explaining about life on earth and how no one really knew where it came from, and how some people thought it started from gases or came off meteorites, when it came to me to say, well, maybe it's like a rockpool. Noah didn't understand what I meant at first so I says it's like how when you've got your hand in a rockpool and all the little shrimps is darting out between your fingers and you know they're just tolerating you and waiting for the tide to come back—maybe there weren't no reason to suppose the earth were any different and once long ago, life got here like how the sea gets to a rockpool and that one day the sea'll come back to carry us off someplace new. Noah didn't say nothing at first and it were like he was thinking hard, and finally he says it were a nice theory but that it couldn't be true for all sorts of reasons and I asked why not and he said because for one thing there weren't no evidence. Proper scientists always wait for evidence before making decisions. But he showed me a book he had what was full of all sorts of stuff about the beginnings of life and told me that everything in there had once only been theories too.

So it were with a clearer idea of scientific procedure that I first come to hear of the magnapinna.

It were about this time last year, the day before we was meant to be leaving for the cottage and Dad showed me a video on his phone that were like nothing I'd never seen before.

What's that? I gasped.

That's called a magnapinna, Dad said, *it's a bigfin squid.*

I was transfixed watching it twizzling round all ghostly white like a puppet with its strings cut and trailing out behind it far off into the empty blue distance. He said that it's one of the first times anyone had ever got a proper video of it and no one was like to get a better one no time soon since it normally lived deep underwater.

Unless you find one down in your rockpools, of course.

And all the way in the car the next day I couldn't stop thinking about what I'd seen and when we got to the cottage I borrowed one of Noah's books about sea creatures but there weren't nothing in it and I realised I must be in what Noah'd call uncharted territory. By the time the Westbys arrived to join us at the cottage a few days later, I'd had time to draw up some diagrams what proposed how long ago, back when we was all living in the sea, we might very well have evolved from the magnapinna. I told Lottie how each night animals what live deep underwater float up to the surface when no one's looking, so if we was hoping to gather evidence about the magnapinna then that were our best opportunity.

Will it do it tonight? Lottie asked, squinting.

It does it every night, I told her gravely, pointing to my calculations.

Oh, let's us go see! she pleaded, hardly able to contain herself. *Please, let's us!*

So that evening while everyone else was gathered round the telly, me and Lottie snuck out the cottage and headed down the coast path to the beach. The tide was way out and the sun was going down over the water making the rockpools glow pink. While I was finding us a good spot to wait, Lottie went off on her own and came back with her arms full of slimy seaweed that she dumped down in a pile beside me.

What you got there?

It's so it don't spot us watching, she explained all breathless and began to put bits over me.

It won't be able to see us no ways once it's dark, I explained, brushing it off.

But I reckon it got good eyesight, she draped the seaweed over me again and began to wrap what was left round her own shoulders, *what with being down under the water all day. I reckon it'll go back down if it sees us waiting.*

I tell you it don't matter.

How'd you know? she demanded, putting her hands on her hips and looking for all I could see of her like some raggedy mermaid stood up on the rocks on her scaly tail, *now you keep that on or it'll go back down I say!*

It was near complete dark when we heard people calling our names and saw four torch beams jostling down the coast path and onto the rocks where we was still sat.

The both of yous had us worried half to death! Don't you know how dangerous these rocks are at night with the tide coming in? And get that rubbish off you before it ruins your dress, girl!

No, Mum, we need it! Lottie protested hugging the seaweed tight to her, or else— I nudged her sharp in the ribs.

I mean… we was just playing.

The door was locked the next night so we couldn't sneak out again. We might have tried a window but I didn't know how we'd ever get back in and then all of a sudden it were time for the Wetbys to go home and me and Lottie were stood watching our parents shake each other's hands and kiss each other on the cheek. Lottie had been all sulky since that night we was caught, but as she were getting into the car she suddenly said, *Why don't you give me a kiss?*

What?

She offered me her cheek. *Go on, it's only gentlemanly.*

So I did. I tried to be as quick as possible so no one else would notice and when Lottie turned away she was smiling all pleased with herself, and I suppose I was feeling pleased with myself too for doing it like she asked, and as I watched the car pulling away I felt all jittery like I had it in me to run after it and keep pace with it no matter how fast it were going, and tap on the window for Lottie to roll it down and climb in beside her and kiss her on the cheek again and tell her how we never had to be away from each other ever again.

And in the months that followed I kept on thinking about Lottie and how this year we'd find a way to sneak out to the beach and see the magnapinna for real and I thought about all the things I'd tell her, like my theory of how the magnapinna had created the world and filled it with life, or how Noah'd got given an award from school and how on parent's evening his teacher said he was doing a right masterous job and how he predicted the best of things for his future. Because he really was doing well and everyone said he was getting bigger and you could hear his voice dropping deeper.

That's my brother, I would tell the other kids proudly whenever we saw him coming home from school, *he's the one to prove my theory!*

But when I tried to explain, they just laughed and somehow Noah heard about what I'd been telling people and one evening he come barging into my room with his glasses all steamed up.

Now you listen here! That there magnapinna's just some dumb squid, ain't the first thing special about it, except its rare. I've a bright future ahead of me and I don't need you messing it up, making me look soft, so grow up and stop this stupidity before you embarrass me anymore! I don't want nothing more to do with none of your stupid theories!

Right now he'll be up at the cottage I reckon, waiting with his deep new voice for the conversation to move in a direction what lets him bring up all he knows about gases, or meteors, or where we all came from, or how there's been a lot of nonsense lately about something called a magnapinna, which wasn't nothing but some boring old squid and that you'd have to be stupid to think otherwise. Lottie'll be listening, even though Noah don't never speak to her, and I know she'll be waiting for a chance to nudge me under the table and ask me about all that he's been saying and about the magnapinna and slowly realising how I'd cooked it all up just to try and impress her and impress Noah and she'll be putting her hands on her hips and saying *You've made me look a right softie!* and that'll be that and she won't never want to see me again no matter how gentlemanly I might be.

So maybe I'll wait here a little longer till the tide comes up over the rocks and pushes me back all the way onto the coast path. But I'll be gone before it gets dark and before the moon sends its reflection down like a kid dipping his fishing net into the water, hoping to fetch up all sorts of mysteries from below.

I REMEMBER
Freya Calcluth

I remember the sad times, the crying and the yelling.
I remember the tantrums and the family fights,
the counselling where they spoke for me
(I didn't know how to speak for myself),
and I'd get angry because they didn't know me.

I don't remember the good times, the laughing times,
the moments caught on camera of me grinning, teeth showing.
I am not the girl I see in those pictures my mother shows me.
In the garden, hair wet, playing with snails,
watching the horses with my cousins.

I don't remember the happy times,
all the times that I wish I could remember, I don't.
I look at the pictures that have been taken of me,
and don't remember the little blonde girl with
her two older brothers, her amazing parents that tried so hard.

But each photo is filtered with regret and sadness
because it is not me anymore.
And I wish, for the life of me, to remember who I was.
But that is the sadness of memories;
we can only remember the things we wish to forget.

PLEASE.
Freya Calcluth

please
do not
let me die
with my head sunk
in lonely memories long gone
and my heart untouched by you

please touch your skin to mine
and whisper into my ear
show me devoted love
i'm too scared
to show
you

THE WAY I'LL DROWN
Freya Calcluth

I wonder if the rocks in my shoes
will cut me or drown me first.
Have they stabbed their way into my feet?
My bloody underfoot squirms in the salt water,
will I scream for help or will I close my eye
to every pain that shadows me?

Or maybe I don't drown in the sea,
maybe in the freshwater river of Deben.
The swans we watched together
can pluck food from my skin.
The wrecked boats could decay
in the waterbed I will never wake from.

Or a swimming pool, where no attendant watches,
And the chlorine poisons my eyes.
I do not feel numb when I go.
Maybe the stinging will stop me,
Allow me to feel every craved pain that I dearly miss.

Asking for pain is better than asking for death, no?
But I think I'll drown, nonetheless.
No pain will stop my need of sinking.
These rocks weigh me down with
blood ribbons in the water.

YOU TELL ME YOU LOVE ME.
Freya Calcluth

You tell me you love me.
I look at you, smiling with tears in my eyes:
I'm scared you won't find happiness in me.

You reassure me;
no sadness or numbness will stop this.
You tell me you love me.

You plan our days and our nights.
I'm too tired to go out. Let me stay in bed.
I'm scared you won't find happiness with me.

I stay in bed for that week, you stay with me.
You hold me, you tell me it will be alright,
and you tell me you love me.

No matter your love language, I still have doubts:
what if I'm breaking you, to fix what's broken in me?
I'm scared you won't find happiness with me.

You promise me it'll be worth the pain,
you will be by my side every step of the way.
You tell me you love me
but I'm scared you'll never find happiness with me.

STEAK DINNER
Georgia Greetham

As Alfie lit the flare for the rescue ship, the rushing sound it made as it spun into the air reminded him of fireworks. When he was younger, his dad would always let him light them, ignoring his mum's pleas to be careful. After a few years, they stopped, his mum claiming the smell of smoke gave her a headache, but he loved it, straining his neck to see the colours explode in the sky. But as much as he had loved those fireworks, they couldn't come close to watching the ship turn around and he saw the flare. After that, he had felt like a flare himself, the rush of adrenaline obscuring any real emotion. As he hugged his tearful mother for the first time, and held his father's hand while he feigned sleep in a hospital bed, nothing had felt real. Instead, there was a distance between him and the real world, a floaty sort of distance that reminded him of dreaming. It wasn't until he had been discharged from the hospital that the feelings had begun to return.

However, so far all he had really felt was the sensation of intense strangeness. Everything, even sitting at their dinner table felt wrong, like it was something a different version of himself would have done. China patterned plates, stained tablecloths, chairs that forced you to sit in a particular way; it felt like a different world to the one he had inhabited only a couple of weeks ago. Even holding a knife and fork felt foreign, as if he was a toddler learning to use cutlery for the first time. He put them down with a little more force than necessary, causing his mum to jump.

"Is something wrong?" She asked, in the lilted, faux-happy voice he had heard her use countless times before.

He shook his head. "Everything's fine, mum."

Judging by the expression on her face, she wasn't convinced. She looked pointedly at his dad, but his attention was too focused on the television screen to pay her any attention. Alfie followed his gaze but blanched when he saw what was playing.

They were talking about the crash again. It was virtually all the news had covered since they had been found, telling the story in thousands of different ways: from how the plane broke to the pilot's medical history and the island they had been found on, every news outlet kept finding new ways to tell the same story. Sometimes, at night, he found himself wishing for a natural disaster or a serial killer to show up, just to take the heat off of him.

Today, judging by the picture of the smarmy looking man in the suit gracing the television screen, they were covering the airline. Alfie vaguely remembered him: he had come to visit him in the hospital, looking significantly more dishevelled than he did in the picture. He had shaken his hand and offered a stiff apology that had felt more like a plea not to sue than any actual concern.

"Henry Crawford, the CEO of Crawford Airlines reportedly stepped down earlier today." The news anchor said. "This comes only two weeks after the survivors of the Crawford Airlines flight 851 were found on a remote island off the coast of Malaysia, after being presumed dead for—"

His mum turned off the television with an authoritative click. Alfie found himself still staring at the spot where Henry Crawford's face had been.

"I was watching that." His dad said, and this time he caught the full force of his mother's glare.

"Enough of that, I think." She said before turning to Alfie, a much softer expression forming. "We're having steak for dinner, if that's okay?" She said, and his mouth went dry. "I know you're doing this whole vegetarian thing, but steak was always your favourite."

He'd been strictly vegetarian ever since he'd left the island. When he'd gotten to the hospital, they'd asked if he had any dietary restrictions, he'd told them without even thinking that he could eat anything other than meat. If his parents had found this strange, they hadn't said anything.

Until now, that is.

His mum served up the steak and he stared at it for a moment. If he focused on something else, like the distant clattering of knives and forks, he could almost dissociate the food in front of him from his thoughts of flesh, blood and meat. But then he forced his knife into it, and couldn't hide his grimace. Almost immediately, he felt his mum's eyes on him.

"What's wrong, darling?"

There was a chunk of steak on her fork, and while she was neglecting it in favour of him, it was all he could focus on. There was a bite-sized chunk taken out of it, with stringy meat bordering the sides. It was pinker on the inside, fleshier too. He could imagine it alive, breaths going up and down at a steady pace like meditation.

It was Mike who had taught him to meditate. For the first few days after the crash, his panic attacks had come back, even worse than they had been when he was younger. Mike had found him one day, leaning against a palm tree and gripping at its roots. Once he'd calmed down, Mike had spent the afternoon teaching him how to breathe again. He'd been a therapist before the plane crash, as he'd told Alfie over a hearty dinner of aeroplane peanuts. He'd also been the only one in his family to survive the crash. They'd had that in common. The next day, the two of them had gone to the crash site, Mike saying a few words about his wife and son, and Alfie saying a few words about his friends. That had been the first day on the island that he'd gone without a panic attack.

"Alfie?" His mum said, and he jerked his eyes away from the cube of meat still dangling from her fork. "What's going on?"

"Nothing." He slammed his fork into an over-boiled potato. It was entirely flavourless, but soft, mushy potato didn't remind him of the metal taste of blood.

He looked up at the heavy sound of a sigh. His mum had put her cutlery down and was looking at him in a final sort of way that she would when he'd come home after curfew.

"Your father and I are worried about you." She said. "You've barely spoken to us, and Doctor Webster told us you haven't been communicating properly in your therapy sessions."

When he said nothing, she turned to his dad, who looked intently focused on serving himself more potatoes.

"Just help us understand." His mum said. "Please?"

He shrugged.

"Mark, can you back me up here please?" His mum said.

"He's fine." His dad said. "Don't push it."

His mum quirked an eyebrow.

"Why don't you try actually asking your son how he's feeling? If you even care, that is."

"There's a difference between caring and mollycoddling, Julie."

"At least make the effort. Or is that too hard for you?"

"What, you think this conversation isn't effort?"

"Can someone pass the salt?"

His parents turned to look at him, surprised. It was as if they had forgotten he was in the room entirely. His mum coughed. His dad passed him the salt.

While he'd been on the island, he'd spent a lot of time thinking about the sort of home he'd return to. It had seemed inevitable at the time, that they'd realise they had only been staying together for him, and by the time he was back they'd be separated. Mike had told him one morning, while they were fishing with makeshift rods, that he had been planning on asking his wife for a divorce once they were home. He'd caught her cheating, he'd confessed as he jabbed the rod just a little too forcefully, with a guy from her office. The only reason he hadn't said anything before the trip was because his son, Zack, had been looking forward to their trip and he didn't want to ruin it for him.

They didn't catch any fish that day.

"I think that's enough salt, dear." His mum said.

He looked down. His steak was now covered in salt, obscuring the meat completely. To him, it felt like an improvement, but under his mother's watchful gaze, he scraped most of it off with his knife. The feeling of meat under the knife made him shudder, but he hid it well.

"Come on, Alfie." His mum sighed. "That doesn't even look edible now!"

"I've had worse." He said it before he had time to think about it. His mum paled, and he forced himself to cut a bite of steak.

As their food had begun to run out, their group had become increasingly desperate. He'd eaten a wild boar that gave him food poisoning, nettles that made his tongue bleed and even tried drinking from the ocean.

He'd always wanted to try that as a kid. He understood now why his mum would never let him.

"If you want something else, I can make it for you." His mum said.

"I'm fine," Alfie said. "I like steak."

To prove his point, he stuck a forkful of meat into his mouth and forced himself to chew, a decision he regretted almost instantly. While the texture of the meat had felt weird under his fork, it was nothing compared to how it felt in his mouth. He didn't understand how he could have ever enjoyed eating this, when it was so stringy and chewy, with bits of animal caught in his teeth. He forced himself to swallow it and took a long sip of water.

Water was one of the few things the crash had been unable to ruin for him. Although the hunger had been bad, the dehydration was torture. As they began to run out of water, their numbers had dwindled dramatically. It was only then that one members of their party had the idea that drinking blood would give them some hydration. It was better than saltwater, but it wasn't a cure-all.

Not all of them had made it.

"Is something wrong with the steak?" His mum asked. "Did I not cook it enough?"

He shook his head. "It's fine, it's cooked."

Mike had fallen unconscious before he passed. It was something Alfie had been grateful for. He had stayed by his side until he took his last, shuddering breath, but he had taken his time in telling the others. Mike was still warm when they returned to him. To a stranger, he would have looked like he was sleeping, but he knew better. Something was missing. He wasn't there anymore. It was just a body.

Alfie wasn't sure who had made the suggestion, but at that point, he was too exhausted to care. He let one of the others prepare it, choosing instead to sit under a palm tree, grip the roots, and focus on his breathing. Someone handed him some of the meat, and he bit into it before he could think about it too hard. It wasn't a nice taste, but he was too hungry to be picky. And if he squeezed his eyes shut and leant against the tree, he could pretend that he was sitting at his dining room table, and this was only steak.

CAPTAIN HOOK WORKS NIGHTS
Grace Bartle

you'd talk of ink-spilled waters.
your cool hands over my ears,
I heard the contending waves.

you'd talk of a crocodile's tick
and a person called Ben,
flying straight on 'til morning.

you said you startled them
and they called you the villain,
but you were just there as a warning.

you'd appear in the nightmares
of the children who thought
that they could fly forever.

you came as a reminder,
lost boys become lost men;
they forget to clap for the fairies.
That's why you always scared them.

MELTED LOLLIES
Grace Bartle

She picks up his baby picture
tracing his strawberry-smudged smile
She's in the picture too
or used to be she's sure

In this scene her boy splays out
centred on a sun-bleached towel
She's jealous that it holds him
and retains his sticky smell

She wonders where this towel is now
because she'd like to smell it
but she knows the picture keeps it
it holds her sweet boy too

TELL ME YOUR FANTASIES
Ingrid Jensen

I have this fantasy where somebody I love slits me open with a box knife, from throat to groin and takes everything out, all my blood, organs, and bones. They take the vertebrae of my spine out singly, carefully, slowly, like they're unpacking a crate of crystal glasses. In my fantasy, they don't go about surgically emptying me, like a doctor. They approach it like a scientist, with a quiet delight and childlike curiosity. When I'm finally empty, just a strip of skin like a cast-off magician's cloak, they pick me up and twist me like a piece of fusilli, until I'm once more an object with enough weight and dimension to be thrown with a purpose. In my fantasy the world is tiny and the person I love is huge. They walk to the top of the globe, towering off it, and hurl me in my new shape into space. I disappear and don't come back, but I don't stop, either. My head's been left intact, remember, so I can still see. I hurtle through black space and stars and nebulas and blue galaxies, and I never stop seeing new things. I just float on.

When he said, *tell me your fantasies*, maybe I shouldn't have said, this.

I have this fantasy where I give birth to the child of my partner, and during the birth, something goes very, very, wrong and I die. The baby's fine, but I die. My partner's holding the baby, he's looking at me like I've just won an Oscar and then beat the head of the academy over the skull with it. Like I've just done something unbelievably wonderful, but he doesn't understand my reaction to it, because if he had done it, his reaction would be different. But then it gets bloodier and bloodier and worse and worse, and nobody thinks to stick me in a tub of ice, which was how Percy Shelley stopped Mary Shelley from haemorrhaging to death. And suddenly it's obvious to him that I'm not walking out of this room, that it's going to be just him and this baby forever. And in this final moment of wavering between life and death, when the whites of my eyes go red and I stop breathing, he stares at me with a look of understanding, of pure horror and guilt. It's the last thing I see, but it's the understanding I've been looking for my whole life. I am finally able to die at peace, venerated, and ecstatic, although I can't show it. After all, I'm out of breath. I'm out of time. But it's still a relief.

Maybe when he said, *tell me your fantasies*, maybe I shouldn't have said, this.

I have this fantasy where I have an out of body experience at a formal event. I go to fix my hair in the powder room, and somebody offers me a line of ket. I say no, thank you, and make a joke about the powder room having a different meaning, now. Then I leave because a sudden mystic feeling has enveloped me. I wander out of the ballroom in a daze, and half an hour later, somebody finds me on the terrace with my eyes rolled back and hair spread out over the tiles like that photo of Jean Shrimpton as the Sun. I look gorgeous, and the girl who finds me is impressed. She goes to get my partner and he's like *whoa, Jesus, fuck!* He's cradling my head, saying, *you ok?* But I'm out of the office, I'm having a vision, I'm looking down and thinking, this is so much better than the absolute shite they show on television. I'm acutely aware that I want him to fuck me, but I can't get back in my body to tell him so. Slowly I work my way back home through time and space. I come to and tell him everything. My partner's mouth drops open and he says, *whoa!* several times. He swallows a large glass of whiskey and feeds me a chicken salad sandwich because he thinks I have low blood sugar. He suggests we leave the party. We take the train home and fall asleep in a tangle on the sofa with our shoes on. I wake up with his hair in my mouth and his cigarette ash down the front of my strapless satin dress. He strokes my hair, and I'm so happy, I think, if it all ends now, it's ok. For fifteen whole minutes, everything is ok.

When he said, *tell me your fantasies*, maybe I shouldn't have said anything at all.

SHE SAID THERE'S A SCORPION IN ME
Jennifer Shen

She said there's a scorpion in me
that we didn't know about
She was feeling her way across my ribcage
"you see we thought its legs to be your ribs"
      i was putting my arms above my head
so She could see the scorpion better
see my scoliosis better
      i was biting my lips hard
      i wasn't supposed to laugh
when She was counting my ribs
      i was lying in our bed, floating in the sea & sky
      i was the patient etherized upon the table
      i was merely The Hanged Man

She was reading me like a stab wound
"the venom has purpled your lips"
She was reading me like a poem
line by line & bone by bone
      i was the sonnet without a couplet
      i was trying to grow another pair

      i was smiling by then.

THE CHICKEN DANCE
Jessica Blissit

I cannot stop staring at her. Her warm brown eyes, puckering lower lip, and elusive smile. She wants me. That face full of shiny dimples and smiles, she looks kind. The kind of woman to raise kids with; to hold at night. I wonder who she's talking to. It's not shown on the magazine, it's like they've cut his head off and rammed on their signature brand logo instead. I think it's an old advert for sandwiches with a company that went bust a few years ago.

Don't move your head, no quick moves. Don't try and be smart here, it won't work out. Keep looking at her.

She's not actually that pretty now that I think about it. When I look at her and the whole pamphlet, a crinkle cut above her eyebrow, she just looks a bit dusty. I should really have dusted underneath there, next to the canned goods. Her smile is just a bit too bright, and with those eyes? You just know that she would have been treated like a spoiled princess her entire life. Plus, her smile has been filled in, probably by those boys from the school down the road. She's vandalised.

Someone's walked in, I can hear them crying a few metres away. Don't focus on them, you can't. Look at the girl. The girl on the pamphlet.

I still don't know why I was so fascinated with her to begin with, or why she caught my eye. She reminded me of someone I met at my brother's wedding. Julie. Yes, she has Julie's smirk, that's why I'm fixed on her. And because…

I met Julie five years before my brother's wedding at a swinger's party, but she didn't remember that until I mentioned it. On a microphone. When I was meant to be toasting the happy couple. The silence that followed was exhilarating, I really shocked them. They wanted her to hit me or run out of the room crying, but she only laughed. She said it was funny and what a new way to introduce myself. That was so Julie, she was always such a people pleaser, she wasn't going to cause a fuss. Pathetic. Plus, I think she liked the attention, and I was particularly charming that day. I wore my lucky boots.

Her laugh was very annoying, it was a little too loud and a little too high-pitched, but I liked that she would always look away when she laughed, like she was embarrassed by how easy it was to make her laugh. After buying her an apology drink (that she begged me to buy her) I took her onto the dance floor. It was a classic move, to show I wasn't entirely uptight. We walked onto the square, and she hitched up her skirt (she had been a bridesmaid) and she danced to the chicken song for two minutes straight. By the end of it, she was an embarrassing sight, flustered and sweaty. I remember hoping she wouldn't be too sticky to kiss later because, from all her panting, this was clearly the most exercise she'd done in a while. I remember this surprised me, because she was as thin as a stick insect. In fact, she had the weight and bone structure of a tiny baby bird, so delicate and fragile. I think that's what I noticed about her first.

I would have usually died of embarrassment if someone pulled me into a frantic dance of the chicken song, but I wanted to impress her, so I stuck it out with the same enthusiasm, and we both pathetically embarrassed ourselves until we crashed onto a nearby couch. I remember her leaning into me then, how she suddenly felt safe around me and I played along for her amusement, as if a chicken dance had won me over. Then, we spoke about our lives and what we'd done since I saw her dangling from that sex swing. I told her I owned a convenience store in the city. She seemed surprised, so I told her it was a family business, how I had grown up shelving items after school, and I couldn't wait to leave school and start working full-time on a full-time salary. I joked about how I had enough money to buy my own apartment and Christmas presents at nineteen, instead of dealing with crippling tuition fees like everyone else my age. At this point, I asked her if she'd gone to university, and she said no, so I thanked her for not being yet another person I had to lecture about the cluelessness of higher education. All it does is delay the inevitable, what everyone depends upon—a secure income.

That's when she told me she didn't have a job. I laughed loudly to begin with, but the joke didn't come and when it didn't, I demanded that she tell me how the hell she paid for anything. I imagined her stripping out of that lilac ball gown in the muddy rain of a motel and covering herself in wet cardboard. She walked away from me then, embarrassed, and ashamed I guess, but I consoled her and told her it was nothing to be ashamed about. It was, but I told her it was a minor dip in the road. Then, I took her by the hand and led her to the balcony of this cheap rec centre. Below, the candles glittered like fireflies, and it felt like we were just out of earshot. We could still have a private conversation and hear every wedding toast if we wanted to. I had been planning on bringing her here at the end of the night for a quick snog, but she clearly needed some comfort, and I needed a way in.

Her lips looked particularly soft and pretty, as she told me that she made enough money to pay for a place to live and food to eat, she just didn't want to be tied down by money. She said she was an entrepreneur, whatever that meant, and that she flew around the world doing odd jobs and never staying anywhere longer than a month. I cradled her face in my hand and asked if she ever got lonely. She paused then, and I wondered how she felt knowing her life, for all intents and purposes, had slipped away from her. She stood up and said at times, but the freedom was too important to give up on. I imagined keeping her with me this weekend and the thrill of kicking her out Sunday morning.

There we sat, brandy in our hands, and we began a flirtatious debate over an old question, and one I was well-rehearsed in: spontaneity or security? It was so much fun, all those flirty little comebacks, I could barely hear anything she said, but I kept leaning closer and closer. I argued that yes, freedom was fun, but what about all the support and love you get from settling down, the chance to start a family, how exhilarating *those* kinds of adventures could be! To be part of a community, knowing your neighbours more than a quick goodbye, making lifelong friends and having a place to call home. Wasn't that what life was all about? We were daring each other, like poised panthers, challenging each other. I couldn't get enough of it. The pretty pink that bloomed in her cheeks from pure ridicule, or the perfectly round poise of shock her face crumpled into when she felt insulted.

She argued that any place could become home, whether you've lived there fifteen years or fifteen minutes, that there were some places you could grow up in for twenty years and never feel like you belonged. I felt like she used an example here, but I can't remember what she said. She argued that those weren't real adventures, and if starting a family was so great, why hadn't I already got hitched. We were inches apart then, almost kissing, but she pulled away, loving the chase.

I couldn't deny her brutal tone towards me left me breathless. There was a fiery stubbornness there, I knew it. And I wondered to myself how it would play out for the evening. What we had was buzzing, so I knew I had to make the first move. I followed her to her hotel room.

Really, it felt like she was leading me up there, she left early and was constantly checking to see if I was still behind her. I gave her a bit of distance; I didn't want to come across as too eager. I thought to myself, this should be fun. Teasing my prey, savouring the hunt. Just as we reached her hotel room, she suddenly lashed out at me. It came from nowhere. She refused to let me in and told me to go and enjoy the festivities. Well I'll be honest, I felt cheated. She had seduced me all night, only to screw me over at the last minute! I felt like I had wasted two hours for nothing. I wanted answers, and her first five excuses weren't good enough, until she finally barked:

"You have done nothing but humiliate me and laugh at my life choices all night! I've been trying to leave for hours, but you haven't let me! Did you really think I was going to sleep with you?'

She laughed at that, but it was a different laugh. A low gurgle dripping in sarcasm and spite. Her tone seemed so pointed, but with such tiny cheekbones and rosebud lips, even her furrowed brow looked adorable. I must have lent in because she slapped me and yelled ---

"You only wanted to sleep with me because you saw what I did in that sex swing!"

And then she slammed the door, like an insolent child. She was pathetically dramatic like that. But I'm starting to think she might have a point. It's funny, I never really heard what she said until now. Until I started staring at this pamphlet. Until today, when someone pointed a gun at my head and told me to empty all the cash out of the register or he would blow my brains out.

I love my store. Every week there's a new sales item and this week we were trying to sell something organic, so I bought pounds of flaxseed. We never sold any, but I can see it in the corner of my eye as I count all the cash from the register. My cash, that I earnt. After this I'll have nothing. I hope I'll value my life more than money, but I can't seem to hand it to him.

Just please, please, please.

Don't shoot me.

YOU TOOK OUR PEACE AWAY
Julian Beacom

It is said that when fear grips your heart, when you have lost everything, the world around you becomes a blur. You become trapped in your own body: seeing, hearing, and feeling everything.

Yet, you're not in control—they've already taken that from you. Instead, it is as if you are trapped beneath the ice—slowly drowning as the world as you know it fades away…

This is how Melina and all the people of Brigadon have felt since the neighbouring Remulian Empire invaded three days ago. Now Melina was on the run, moving through the untamed mountainous region of her homeland in search of a city, a town, even a village that was not raided, besieged, or destroyed.

"Tarsdorf is only a few hours away now," said one of the villagers she had fled with. Altogether, Melina had left her village, Vralas, alongside thirty-seven others when news reached them that the people of the capital city had all been slaughtered by the Remulians.

When smoke began to rise from the farmsteads that marked the outskirts of the village, they knew they had to either run or die. *'I choose life…'* Melina thought to herself, shoving away the feeling of her stomach rumbling its complaints. Instead, the auburn-haired girl decided to focus on the conversations around her, to distract her.

"The Remulians probably came from Tarsdorf. They've controlled Worgel and Linze in all but name for the last century after all," said Syla, her village's resident alchemist. Syla was the person who knew the most about the world outside of Brigadon, for she was someone who moved into the duchy rather than was born here.

Melina always thought Syla was mad. Why would anyone move to Brigadon? The nation was oppressed by the Remulian Empire who first demilitarised the nation on the threat of complete subjection otherwise. When that was not enough, they placed armies at the cities that bordered the Empire, *'for protection'* Melina remembered her mother saying. She hated that word now. There was no protection against an Empire who stole every ore her people mined and who now carve a path of death and destruction through a country who have no defences, no real army.

"If Tarsdorf has fallen, then we will head further west to Ennes then. We could catch a ship—" suggested a farmer, Cyrus, only to be quickly silenced by his wife.

"Even if the Empire did not burn every ship at Ennes, we'd have no friendly waters to go to. Sail west and we pass the Empire's land. Sail east and we sail across raider lands."

Melina closed her eyes briefly as the group continued their trek, her mind spinning from the desperate plans her neighbours made. They avoided the official roads, sticking to older—and less known—dirt paths that ran through the crags and forests of Brigadon.

Yet, there was no real escape. To the west, lay the path towards the border with the Empire while to the east was where they fled from. They could go north, if they had ships to sail and even then, there were no friendly waters. South… South was not a real option either, not anymore.

Melina didn't realise that her breath had become shaky, nor did she realise when her body gave out and crumpled to the ground. She didn't feel any pain, her body just felt numb, disconnected from everything.

It was only when hearing Syla's voice and feeling two strong arms lifting her up quickly that her mind snapped back to reality. Blinking a few times, Melina looked around at the others before her vision was covered by Syla dabbing a cloth across her forehead.

"She's getting weaker without food…" Syla said with a sigh as she looked towards one of the men holding Melina up.

"Then she is like the rest of us," he says in a low grumble. There was no malice in the man's voice, simply that of someone who had given up hope as well.

"She's nineteen Marko and has been in shock since we had to run away without her parents."

Melina gulped at the mention of her parents. She opened her mouth to speak yet found no words to say. Instead, she closed her mouth softly and shrugged off the assistance to walk on her own again. At first, the young girl stumbled—her strength still sapped by shock—but she kept going.

'Your father is too sick to travel my dear and I will not leave him alone…' Melina's mother had told her when the villagers started to flee. Most did not take anything with them, only what they could grab in a hurry. 'Go and live a life for the two of us instead. Get away from this hell Melina.'

Her mother's last words were still hammered into her mind. Melina was certain it was the only thing staving off the hunger and fatigue that was slowly chipping away at her body. *'I will mama… I will get away.'*

As the sun began to set, the group of weary refugees reached a crossroad. Melina was not sure how long they had been travelling for, but this crossroad meant that their journey would hopefully be over soon.

It was here that a decision would finally need to be made: one road led towards Tarsdorf, Brigadon's main agricultural and commercial centre; the other would lead them towards Ennes, the only port town left in Brigadon.

While the others decided where to go, Melina took the chance to finally have some rest. Walking through the golden-brown grass, she took a deep breath and enjoyed the fresh spring air.

Brigadon was always a beautiful place in her eyes, Melina loved wandering the golden fields of wheat around her village or sitting by the lake as it thawed in the first days of spring.

Life had been idyllic and simple, and, for a moment, a smile crept across Melina's lips at the memory. Yet, the smile soon faded. That life felt like an entirely different world now, it was the first casualty of this invasion.

Finding a place to sit on a small boulder, Melina sighed slowly. It felt as if her body was filled with pins and needles the moment she sat down, all the fatigue and stiffness from countless hours of travelling finally caught up with her. She felt as if her body had decided to fall asleep there and then.

Taking another deep breath, Melina's eyes went wide. The fresh spring air suddenly had hints of smoke weaving through it—burning Melina's nostrils with the scent. Looking around, Melina opened her mouth to speak —only for the screams of others to fill the air instead.

From the direction of Tarsdorf, there was suddenly a wave of people coming from the horizon. The lucky ones raced past Melina and her group on wagons or horseback. However, most were running for their lives as black plumes of smoke rose behind them—closely followed by mounted Remulian Soldiers firing arrows and slashing indiscriminately at the citizens.

"Melina—Melina!! Come on, we need to go! Run!" Syla yelled, grasping the girl's arm and dragging her away towards the direction of Ennes. The rest of the villagers were already fleeing as well—some stumbling over in panic while others did their best to pick their neighbours up and help them.

Yet, Melina was simply left stunned, watching the raiders advance. Those who were wielding torches, flung them across the fields of grass, setting the golden-brown fields ablaze and further narrowing the paths of escape.

Finally, Melina snapped out of her shock. Exchanging a desperate glance with Syla, both began to run, hand-in-hand, as if providing each other the courage and strength to run and live.

They did not get far. The yells of the raiders and the fleeing civilians drew closer and closer until their horses rushed past Syla and Melina heading towards Ennes. Yet, the two women were still not safe. Syla suddenly stumbled over, causing Melina to fall to the ground as well. Letting out a scream of pain, an arrow had pierced the alchemist's thigh.

Moving towards Syla, Melina looked at the woman helplessly, trying in vain to drag Syla to her feet. "Mel—Melina please… You need to go on without me…" Syla gasped, slowly standing on her feet as she looked around as three riders turned back and began to charge at the two women.

'This is it…' Melina thought to herself, stunned as she stared at the incoming riders. Holding her breath, Melina closed her eyes and waited to meet her fate…

A second passed, then five more. The thunderous thumping of the horses drew closer and closer. Yet, they never reached the pair. Instead, the shriek of horses deafened Melina while the ground shook violently around her.

Opening her eyes, Melina gasped as she saw pale blue-hued energy spiralling around her and coming from Syla. The alchemist stood a few metres in front of Melina, arms raised to either side as a barrier of arcane magic had sent the riders flying backward and smashing across the ground.

"Melina… I cannot… hold them off for long…" Syla gasped out, her voice strained from concentrating on the spell. In the distance, more riders began turning back at the sight of Syla's magic display.

Melina remained stunned, staring at Syla. It was the first time she had ever seen magic in a true form, this was more powerful than the parlour tricks most travelling mages showed in Brigadon.

"Mel... RUN!" Syla screamed, her voice straining even more. The scream was all it took for Melina to snap back to reality again. Blinking a few times, Melina began to sprint away—not to Ennes, not to Tarsdorf, but back the way they came. It was her best chance, or, at least, she hoped it was.

She kept running even as the sound of more and more riders started to echo behind her. Melina kept on going even as she heard more magic booming behind her and Syla letting out a scream.

'I will get away... I will get away... I will—' Melina's thoughts were suddenly interrupted as she crumpled to the ground. At first, she was not sure what happened, only that her body started to feel more and more numb by the second.

Yet, as she looked across her body, Melina spotted an arrow jutting out of her abdomen. She wanted to scream in pain, yet, she felt none and nor could she muster the strength to even say a word. Instead, Melina just felt herself slowly slipping away, watching as the fields around her burned and the cries of her people slowly grew quieter.

In this moment, she felt as if she were disconnected from her body—watching her fate unfold, while she sank deeper and deeper into darkness...

As darkness slowly enveloped around Melina, she saw a light. It was small, no bigger than a child's fist—no stronger than the flicker of a candle. Then it started to grow, blossoming around her into a strange yet seemingly feminine figure.

At this point, Melina was sure she was dead or at least seeing hallucinations in her last moments. Was her mind trying to grasp for hope? Or perhaps yearning for comfort? She was not sure.

"Rise Melina..." a voice emanating from the light spoke. Through those two words alone, Melina felt refreshed—as if new life was being pumped into her veins. "This is not your time. You may choose your own path now."

It did not take long for Melina to decide. She reached out to grasp the hand the figure offered. "I... chose life..." Melina said. These were the first words she had spoken in days yet, they were filled with confidence and newfound power—magic. And then, everything went black.

OFF THE RADAR
Kathy Floyd

She wraps the fleece scarf around her face, ties it tight at the back. A stench like rotting fruit seeps through as she kneels on the floor. She places the bundle and the soiled dressing gown into the sacks, tucks Marcus up on the armchair under her hoodie. Just me and you now babe, she says.

*

The Council found Meg a temporary place when the babies were born — a room in a Victorian terrace opposite the new sheltered housing complex with its white lacy curtains, wood-panelled porches, and composite doors. The entrance to her bedsit was at the side of the house down a passageway. The double-buggy the social worker had found her didn't fit through the door because the folding mechanism had broken, so she would leave it in the front garden under a plastic shower curtain to keep off the rain. That was the last time she had seen anyone from the Services—their Most Updated Communication Introducing Virtual Home Visits lay sealed in a brown envelope undisturbed on the doormat, underneath a flyer telling her Equity Release could be the answer to her problems and six editions of The Weekly Norwich Advertiser.

One morning, when she went outside, the buggy had gone. She walked the length of her side of the street, stopping to look behind rusting cookers, fridges, and broken-down trampolines that had taken root in front gardens. She knocked on doors, but no answers came. An old lady opposite pulled back her curtain and gave her a smile and a wave.

She left the twins in the wooden playpen with the TV turned to full volume and started making necessary visits to the One Stop alone.

One Friday, at the end of the month, her card was declined.

'Seems benefits are going in late for everyone,' the new boy had said from behind the screen. He'd given her the eye. She knew that look. Knew what it could lead to. Still, it made her feel alive and able to forget for a few minutes.

She unzipped the side compartment of her purse, took out the neatly folded five-pound notes she had saved to top up the meter and her phone. She slid them across the counter, paid for the powdered milk, vodka, and frozen burgers, then put the packet of nappies back onto the shelf as she left.

As she stood at the sink mixing the formula with her eyes fixed on the crumbling brickwork of the passageway, a sudden wind whipped at the window. The metal frame rattled, then settled. It continued in this manner throughout the night.

She placed the vodka bottle and her mug on the fold-up table next to the bed and spread out her bath towel. She cut it into four triangles. She pulled the towelling tight over the bellies of her babies, fastening it at the front with hair scrunchies.

Marcus lay on his back, gurgling, amusing himself with the lump at his belly, stretching and contracting his inquisitive fingers over the curiosity. Thomas rolled onto his stomach, thrashed his legs about, beat at the linoleum floor with his clenched fists. She bent down, tried to stuff the dummy back in but he couldn't suck enough with his cleft lip to make the thing stay put.

Thomas would have screamed through every night and day had she not given him a little vodka in his milk. She begrudged this sometimes, especially when her money and the drink was nearly out, but the short-lived respite offered her, those either side of her, and above her, brief moments of quiet.

She came to realise that her babies would have to stay indoors until they could walk, as there was no way she would be able to carry them both to the shop, or anywhere else, for that matter.

But as the days rolled on, she started to miss the remarks and attention, the small talk at the bus stop where the ladies from the sheltered housing waited for the Number 8. They seemed to no longer notice her when she passed by, huddling together in their pointy masks like a family of quacking ducks.

So she began taking one baby out with her. She carried Marcus high up on her hip and the old folk started noticing her again. No-one asked where the other baby was. And nobody said things anymore like, what a shame, how sad, poor little thing, surely something can be done?

Maybe they didn't remember her, or the deformed baby. Sometimes they were so enthralled with Marcus, his perfect face, his life affirming responses, that they didn't notice their bus passing by behind them.

Thomas was the reason the couple living above banged on their floor every night and put notes through her door, which said things like, *Shut that fucking kid up*. And Thomas was the reason the man next door threw his dog's shit over the fence. He was a short man with a large belly which hung down over an elasticated waist like a half-deflated balloon. It was tattooed in a circle the circumference of a football: *MADE IN NORWICH ONE OF A KIND*. She had seen him throwing shit from a trowel onto her path one morning when she was emptying her bin.

*

It was half-eleven on the evening of Guy Fawkes when she heard the sirens coming closer. Thomas had been dead for three days. She was standing at the end of the passage in her dressing gown, thinking, rocking Marcus in her arms, looking toward the end of the shared back garden, watching the smouldering remains of an abandoned fire. The fireworks had upset Marcus. She'd tipped a little Vodka into his milk and within ten minutes he was asleep and limp in her arms.

Climbing into the wardrobe, kneeling, she pulled the door closed, and waited. One hand was pressed over her mouth and nose, the other held Marcus at her breast. She swallowed the bile that rose in her throat. Hot gushing urine stung the insides of her clenched thighs and her bowel emptied itself unashamedly.

She must have stayed there for twenty minutes or so, pressing her nostrils closed tight, breathing in as little as possible through her mouth until the sirens of the ambulance, or maybe it was a police car, faded away.

She was off the radar.

At the One Stop the woman was pulling down the shutters. Meg grabbed black sacks, sanitary towels, Febreze, and two cans of Fosters. She pushed her card into the machine, her finger shook as she keyed in the numbers. The woman leaned back against the tobacco cupboard, folded her arms. I've a good mind to report you, she said, coming in here, thinking you can get away with it.

She looked up at the woman, then down, pulled her card out of the machine, dropped her purse on the floor, and crawled along to gather up the coins. The woman pushed her face through the hole in the Perspex screen, said, If you cut down on your drinking, maybe you could afford to buy yourself a bloody mask like the rest of us.

*

Just me and you now, Meg repeats, tucking her hoodie under Marcus's sleeping body. She locks the door, carries the junk mail and sacks barefoot over the damp grass toward the dying fire.

The polyester dressing gown invigorates the embers, sudden sharp darts of gold and orange shoot through the fabric. She holds her palms at the flames until she can bear it no longer. She pushes the papers into the hot angry tongues that flare and tease and swallow.

The bundle is lighter than before. Maybe because the water he had slipped and drowned in had somehow drained from his body over the hours and days. Had she been sleeping? Was the volume up on the TV so loud that she didn't at first hear the unfamiliar shrieks of Marcus, which eventually drew her to the bathroom? She can't remember. After it happened she couldn't think what she'd done with her towel, so she had pulled the sheet from her bed and wrapped it around the lifeless baby. She'd placed the bundle at the back of the wardrobe, covered it with the pillows from her bed, turned on Big Brother, drank, and tried to think about what was happening.

She'd found Thomas face up in the water, his hands and feet floating freely above it, his cleft lip just breaking the surface like a fish mouth caught in a hook. Marcus was standing up, for the first time, holding onto the edge of the bath, not crying but squealing with satisfaction.

She holds the rigid bundle to her chest. Out here the smell of it is more bearable. Damp earth and rotting leaves seem to embrace the perishing corpse. The fire is blazing higher now, flames dance erratically, scraps of junk mail float up and disappear into the night sky. A rocket goes off in the distance, but she doesn't hear it.

THE ANGEL
Kyle Wakefield

When writers write, they write to dream salvation to their pain,
Stone angels to their liquid souls and marks to mark each Cain.
When painters paint the angels, they paint arms that can embrace,
And bodies that fit into theirs and faces they can face,
And cosseted and princely airs, made smaller by their King's,
And curls to smooth eternal minds and down to soften wings.
With hands that held my human hands and lips for human hymns,
The angels pens invent and brushes paint found flesh in him.

His hair was spun gold in the air and emerald in the tide;
His black eyes sparkled when he laughed and smouldered when he cried.
He had a lily body and a mouth that Millais drew
And the sweet face of an angel that the fist of God went through.

A fever drank up all his blood, made magma of his stone;
His body swelled and buckled with the growing of his bones.
His carcass filled with crimson light which shone out of the cuts,
And tattooed him all over with the shadows of his guts.
Like maggots, feathers furred his back and burst between his ribs,
And with black blood, a voice like death came bubbling from his lips.
The last words that the angel said were, *"Oh, my God, it hurts,"*
And then his red wings ate him like the Great Flood ate the earth.

You look just like an angel, love, means *I see you in stone;*
Your body is my blanket and your shadow's shaped like home.
I worship at your lap, my love, and pray into your mouth;
You're soft and yet steadfast enough to keep an army out.

It doesn't mean *Your eyes, my love, eat light like neutron stars;*
You hack and spatter words; your throat is hollowed raw by fire;
Your wings beat holes into the clouds and shear up roads and trees;
The air around you runs with colours human eyes can't see;
You're larger than the universe, skew orbit with your breath,
Yet smaller than the pathogens which bloom madness and death;
You're always looking at my soul no matter where I turn,
But I cannot look back at you. It burns. It burns. It burns.

THE DEVIL
Kyle Wakefield

        With golden sunlight in Her hair and blue sky in Her eyes,
          The Devil's coming to this earth was cleverly disguised.
        Through twenty beds Her mother's blood the Devil's birth did soak,
          But picking Christian parents was the Devil's little joke.
        When first I met the Devil in Her garden, She was three;
    Her father watched Her toddle, said, "She's plotting something—see?"
          I saw Her pick a clematis and put it in Her hair,
           And, on account of being six, I grimly said, "Yes, Sir."

When first I met the Devil, I was soon to turn nineteen,
And She was old as time itself, or so She made it seem.
Her eyes were black, the velvet kind that makes romantics nervous—
The kind that looks like deep intrigue, not Hell upon the surface.
Her hair was like a lion's mane, wind gusting in its spell;
She smiled with one side of Her mouth and laughed like silver bells.
The bar She found me in was where I went to drink and cower;
She liked to weave Her garlands from the stubbornest of flowers.

        She panted like a dog in church and struck Her head in prayer
          And spoke in tongues and flamed Her eyes with fine dramatic flair.
        Her father was as choked by God as She was choked by Satan,
          So Holy war was pissing contest waged by equal cretins,
        But brainsick eyes and blood-red mouth with long withdrawn canines
          Did hurtle Her past beautiful, and straight into sublime.
        For that which so enraptured me I blame the kin and priests
          Who first engorged Her vanity by calling Her the Beast.

I was a mouse which quivered, shimmered fright from every pore,
But when She asked if I could sing, I sang till I was sore.
She never broke Her gaze with me, Her black, devouring stare;
She drank my song in one long breath and made me gasp for air.
You say the Devil fed on you the way She fed on me?
Her hungry mouth followed my words and found my own with glee.
She chastised me with clear blue eyes and praised me with Her tongue,
And lavished kisses on my throat still aching from the song.

        The Devil fed on me the way the Devil fed on you—
          She sucked my blood and satiation turned Her black eyes blue—
        But with my flesh drawn dry as bone, She tired of me and vanished,
          And left me warring fear of death with hunger to be ravished.

> The hunger itched and burned and took a hundred years to slough,
> But fell away with laughter when I heard She fell in love.
> You think you love a woman, by the public demonised?
> I'm blessed to know I only loved the vice She symbolised.

Sleep smouldered with delirium when first from me She drank;
I woke not sure where my flesh stopped and Devil's flesh began.
She breathed fire through my veins and drew me up in Her embrace,
Sang lullabies and kissed my heart and all around my face.
My mouth She pressed against Her breast; Her blood was warm and sweet—
She moans when She is eaten just as much as when She eats.
My only pain is thinking clear with all Her handprints on,
And walking with an aching belly full of sirensong.

> I've had Her thrice and every time, She butchers me in bed;
> She drinks my soul without a kiss by twisting off my head.
> Her hunger turns the world to blood and chokes blue eyes with blackness,
> A pestilence sans purpose but to clot the meek with madness.
> They say you tried to leave Her once. You made it down the street
> Before the distance cut your strings and slumped you in your seat,
> And when the Devil found the car and put you on Her shoulder,
> The people thought you were a corpse, a fortnight dead or older.

"Come on, my love, let's get you home; don't cry, don't try to speak,"
She said, and stroked my broken limbs and kissed my sunken cheek.
If I'm a dead thing like they say, a Necromancer's toy,
I am the most beloved thing the Devil has destroyed.
She poured Her blood into my wounds, which turned Her blue eyes black;
She drinks from scores but only I will get the blessing back,
And only I will kiss those eyes where blues and storm-clouds bevel.
In all of space-time only I have loved and kept the Devil.

THE NOT GARDEN
Kyleigh Taylor

The Garden was not really a garden. Not in the true sense of the word. While it did have much luscious greenery, and blooming flowers of every color imaginable, it was not a garden.

The Not Garden had sprung up one day out of thin air. Situated in the craggy, gated off hollow between two old and long-since abandoned stucco buildings in the middle of a long-since abandoned small town—forgotten, as Midwestern small towns are wont to—the Not Garden bloomed. No one was around to see it, but if they were, the Not Garden's creation would have been described as a blink. A hiccup. One second there was only stucco and cracks and dust—the occasional weed—and the next minute there was the Not Garden, looking like something out of a fairy tale. Perhaps what some religious folk would imagine the Garden of Eden, though the Not Garden was not a garden.

It spiraled up thirty feet in the air. Long trees like stretched taffy drawing Heavenward, comical, almost, in their physics. Trees that weren't any type of tree at all. Or perhaps they were them all, coniferous, deciduous, the lot, all crammed together. Trees hanging with ivy of impossible colors, blues and purples and pinks and oranges, exploding with flora that reached down into the Earth. The roots of the trees crawled across the hollow, never leaving its confines, but burrowing into the walls of the buildings, criss-crossing over each other and the other plants—bushes delicate as stained glass, ferns larger than life, patches of plump fruit and vegetables—and spooling downward into some unseen depth.

There was no life in the Not Garden.

Animals could be seen in the Not Garden, if one stood at its entrance and stared in. Strained their eyes against the shadows of its foliage and splendor. Looked out from their peripheries, blinked one time too fast. Yellow slitted eyes, the curve of a shoulder, the wave of a tail. Fantastical animals straight from a children's tale. Coyotes with three sets of teeth and winged amalgamations of hooves and beaks and deer with horns ridged down their spine like spindles. Magical animals that would not be amiss from Genesis or Grimms'. Lurking just out of sight between the plants and never visible in the fullest sense, but there all the same. Calls and cries could be heard in the dead of night—assuming there were ears nearby to listen—from sunset to rise: lilting songs of splendor, jubilee, and curious adventure. Beckoning caws and inviting growls. Sounds no normal animals could make without tearing their vocal cords to shreds. Musical sounds that oozed from between the rusting gate that was once an empty hollow but was now a Not Garden.

No one knows when the Not Garden was discovered. Perhaps by some lost travelers, turned around roadtrippers, unsure of their location but weary after miles of vast, empty country roads. Perhaps they saw the signs and prayed for civilization. Perhaps they were looking for a rest stop. A toilet. Food. Whatever it was, whenever it was, and whoever they were, the Not Garden welcomed them. Took them into its arms and cradled them as a babe. Perhaps they were enchanted by its beauty, its whimsy. Perhaps they stayed for hours, days, years. Perhaps they did not want to leave, and yet, they must have, for after its discovery—whenever it was—the Not Garden was known. No longer a space separate from reality, as all things previously unperceived are.

The Not Garden became a sensation. Whispered about in school cafeterias, between cubicles, in strip mall parking lots—everyone and their mother knew of the Not Garden, the eccentricity of its mystery. Some drove hours to find it. None ever succeeded. Despite this, the tale of the Not Garden spread wildfire quick down the American Midwest. How the garden was not a garden, and yet its flowers smelled so sweet—like ambrosia and honey milk and nostalgia. How the food grown between those two stucco buildings was better than any other. The freshest vegetables, the most decadent fruit. How the animals of the garden danced in the shadows of the ghost town, something straight out of a movie, ballroom waltzes and swings as lively as new love.

No one, however, could name a single person who had actually *seen* the Not Garden. This did not stop people from whispering. This did not stop people from believing. This did not stop people from seeking, regardless of their blindness to the Not Garden's favorite rule.

The Not Garden is not found.

The Not Garden finds.

If one was so bold, they could call the Not Garden a savior. It was everything one could ever need. A friend. A parent. A lover. It could make all your worries disappear, soothe a balm over the soul, kiss loneliness away as a mother kisses the scrapes away. Fear would never dare exist in the garden, strangled before it had the chance to run, devoured by a gaping, drooling maw before it could scream; all was peaceful in the Not Garden. It was said that if you were lost, you should call to it. Lost amongst the roads and fields and empty, long-abandoned buildings where only corpses live. GPS malfunctioning or map incorrect. It was said that if you prayed, it could heal any ailment, grant any wish. All you had to do was allow yourself to be found.

Of course, if anyone ever was, no one heard anything about it. This did not stop people from whispering. This did not stop people from believing. This did not stop people from praying, despite the truth of its very being.

Just remember, some said, that if you ever find yourself there, before incomprehensible greenery and mythical beings and stucco walls, crumbling at the seams, just remember one, simple thing. If you find yourself bewitched and pushing back the rusting gate with a creak of unused joints. If the lost whisper in your ears and you step once, twice, three times until the gate clangs shut behind and the sun cowers away, bathing you in the dusty darkness of the garden.

The Garden is not really a garden.

THE BUTCHER OF BELARUS
Laurel Brown

It had been eating away at her for hours on end. A scratching sensation that emerged from the torn layers of her stomach that its claws once called home. It had clutched desperately to the small pieces of skin that it could grasp, using them as fragile support to heave itself into the depths of her mind where it decided to sit complacent for the rest of her shift. A silent presence: one that existed within the dull ache in the pit of her stomach and the weight that lent on her mind. A gentle reminder of its unmoving presence. It would continue to sit there; docile and patient until she gave in. Until she would present it with what it yearned for. The stubborn cravings refused to leave.

It had completely consumed her mind—a triggered avalanche that had her buried six feet under. The pressure was all she could focus on; she grew more distracted with each silent movement of the clock and, although her mind wandered, it returned within the next minute or two. She felt as if she was being strung up, a rope laid snug around the skin of her wrists pulling her in any way it wished. She wiggled and pulled, in a desperate attempt to release herself from the manacles it had placed her in. But to no avail, she would not be able to escape until it was satisfied. It was relentless with a drive to control that was unwavering, hidden beneath the layers of its desire. Yet, she seemed to mind extraordinarily little, for she too desired the same thing. She had found peace in its cruelty.

Maybe that's what brought her to make such a hasty decision—a simple google search brought her to the closest place to satisfy the monster inside. A Butcher's Shop. A quick glance formed a plan and an opinion—it wasn't far away and, although a bit grubby looking from the outside, it would serve to rid of the uncomfortable presence. It seemed to be a small sacrifice for the peace she had been denied for such a prolonged period. It seemed to be the perfect idea; she just wanted some steak.

The exhaustion was relentless, it boxed at her mind continuously, refusing to seize even when she tried so desperately to focus on the road ahead. When she thought it was over, another punch would find its target causing her lashes to flutter quickly; an attempt to keep her strained eyes open and alert. But she refused to lose another round, and as the green light of the dashboard clock read 6.38 pm, she pulled into the dimly lit and secluded street which held the chosen shop. The street itself had a beautiful sort of unsettlement around it; broken streetlights and silence loomed over her as the gentle clack of her shoes on the pavement seemed all that louder. It was peaceful but chaotic, it caused the heart that beat frantically in her chest to mellow into a gentle rhythm but made the palms on her hands grow damp with dripping anxiety. It was like she had company but was still being followed. It lingered.

However, the shop was now in sight: a small box building that sat on the corner of the street. It was neutral in colour, loud enough to make it noticeable but quiet enough to be easily forgotten. The paint was peeling at the corners, like an acrylic painting that was slightly too overdone; the chucks of skin that once adorned its flesh now falling off with each slight contact. A pile of its skin lay lifeless between the pieces of glass and trash that were abandoned on the pavement beneath. It was alive in a sense. It seemed to expand with each inhale and shrink again with a gentle sigh. It caught her interest within how lifelike it was. It attracted her with its aura but repulsed her with the wariness that its appearance brought. Where the windows were usually lined high with bright adverts to catch attention, it was instead barren and riddled with a brownish mould that lined each corner. The vibrant sign that once stood proud above the entrance was now hanging by one arm and was missing several parts of its name. It had clearly lost its identity a long time ago. But still, she continued.

However, it seemed to have kept its identity as she stepped through its mouth into the inside. The gentle ring of its bell-like voice announced her arrival to whoever lay within. Its breath smelt like newly washed sheets or the smell of a bleached bathroom; it was chemically fresh. An aroma that was both pleasing and disconcerting; a paradox to the senses. This paradox continued, for the inside was beautiful, a perfectly constructed sea of innocent white counters that shone under the gleaming yellow lights, while the scent of disinfectant escaped them with each gentle exhale. Inside, the walls did not crack yet layer together perfectly, the gentle colours complimented each other and held on tight; they never let the other crack or peel. Here, posters embellished the walls; the advertisements were clear and stood proudly for what they represented. Their voices were a cacophony of sound all saying something different but when it reached her ears it all seemed to sound exactly the same. It merely wanted to entice her, to push her to take the last step in fulfilling her cravings, and it had succeeded.

The Butcher that stood behind the counter reflected the shop perfectly, on the outside they looked worse for wear. They wore an apron that was once a bright white but was now reduced to an off-white colour from the layers of dirt and grime that encased it, but it seemed to fit them perfectly. When paired with the bespectacled unblinking eyes they were a sight to see, an unsettling one but a sight, nonetheless. The bloody cleaver that was once clasped tightly in his hands was now discarded on the counter; the concentration that was held on their face was now masked with an overly enthusiastic smile. Their attention was placed solely on her.

They were unlike their outward appearance; where they looked downbeat and dirty, they seemed to emanate a brighter aura. They possessed a clean character, a friendly spirit, and a positive attitude. It was refreshing, to say the least. They seemed to enjoy talking to her, they listened intently as she described just what she wanted; they wanted to get it right. Soon, they held out a firm hand with a taster of exactly what she was looking for, at that point it seemed rude to refuse such a generous offer. It passed her lips in a hurried fashion; she couldn't have swallowed it quicker if she tried, the taste did anything but disappoint. Each movement of her jaw gave her a new wave of pleasure, a sort of pleasure that brought an onslaught of satisfaction after it. The beast that lay within her had finally got a taste of the blood it had dreamed of, but it never expected what would be within it.

It began momentarily, a dull thump that hit the side of her skull every couple of seconds. Thump. Thump. Thump. She chose to ignore it, for it wasn't unusual for her to develop a headache after a long day, but the unease of the situation remained. Her eyes soon grew heavy, a weight sat on each eyelid begging for them to be pulled down, to finally close as they so wanted to. Her throat grew bone dry, a rough sandpaper texture that made every movement send a tsunami of pain through her body. The worst of all was the darkened spots that began to cloud her vision and the fatigue that held her body tightly. She was losing control, but still, that euphoric smile stubbornly remained painted on her lips. She had got what she wanted.

An image appeared in parts, a light that seemed a distance away now lay directly in front of her eyes; she could see it. The overwhelming stench of chemicals overwhelmed her fragile nose; she could smell it. The remnants of what was the best thing she had ever eaten remained on her tongue; she could taste it. Somewhere in the distance, a humming sound evolved into the lyrics that her sluggish brain recognized as an old favourite of her mother's. They asked her to dream of them and she promised without hesitation. The picture had woven itself together, each little piece allowed her to see what lay before her. Yet it did not allow her to make sense of the memory that floated just outside of her reach. So, as the Butcher wrapped a moist hand around her waist and pulled her to her feet, all that left her chapped lips was an onslaught of gratitude. They spoke gently of how she had passed out, from what they did not know, but they promised they had helped her in any way possible. Their exact words were that they had 'lifted some weight off her shoulders' and for that she was eternally generous.

She stumbled in their grasp, feeling slightly heavier on the left side of her body but she was regaining her balance and strength with each tentative step she took. It wasn't long before she caught sight of the beautifully packaged meat that lay on the side. They said they'd taken extra special care of it and there it sat, clad in a dress of brown paper and finished perfectly with a bow of string. It was all that she had yearned for the whole day and now it was finally here. The Butcher, smiling gleefully at her happiness, declined her offer of payment claiming instead that she 'had paid enough already'. That in itself made little sense, but she replied with a gentle but enthusiastic smile and thanked them for their time and gratitude. It was then that she took it within her left hand, clutching the meat carefully to her chest while the excitement brimmed out of every pore.

Her feet stumbled blindly after one another as she made a haste exit for the door, pausing only once to look back at the entrance of the shop; at the sign that had once hung by one arm. The sign now sat proudly with two strong arms that supported its weight perfectly, the name of the shop was now coherent: 'The Body of Belarus' it read. It was the best butcher shop she had ever been to and it had only cost her an arm.

LOVE IS A HOT AND COLD WAR
Lidia Lassed

When I see footprints on the white plain,
I know she's passed by,
Timid and calm, all she knows is pain,w
And those heavy snowflakes, in my palm they dry.

"You're too fiery" she shouted,
When I embrace her too tightly, she burns away,
"Leave me alone" she said and departed,
See you next year or another day.

All that's left is a barren land,
People cannot breathe anymore,
That's my fault and I wish you could understand,
I just don't care about you or your planet anymore,

I was freed from my chain a long time ago,
Now I'm limitless and there's only space for my ego.

03:11
Lily Fitzgerald

I can still remember the way the landline felt as I pressed it against my cheek, submerged in a cloud of only four hours of sleep. The receiver's cold, black body, digging its way into my face, clawing onto my skin as my knuckles turned white. My tongue tasted like bile and metal. The scent of my house seemed suddenly too strong, as if my own hallway had become infected by the words that struggled out of the mouth on the other end of the line. They were like cobwebs dangling from the ceiling, like nails sticking out of the floorboards. I asked how long it would be until there was any more news. She didn't know. My tongue tasted like bile and metal. My face had silently become an ocean before I even had time to remember what crying was. Something about the doctors are doing everything they can and still early and fourteen stitches. My eyes had not yet adjusted to the night's blackness. I am out of chronology. I reached to turn on a light, but my arm wouldn't move. I asked when I could visit him. My tongue tasted
like bile and metal.

BURY ME IN THE CREEK
Lucy Cundill

dusty skyline speaks like a traveller, she knows
the earnest nature of the earth and loves
the mildew like a mother; flowers fly off like moths,
cornflower petal wings cast ashadow in the long
rolling sunset, in search of that blue moon crocheted
into the tumbling sepia horizon; heaven looks like mint leaves,
freshly picked and brewed into tea; the peace is here is palpable,
a steady beating heartbeat, part equally of the sky, the ground,
and the trees; there is humanity in the dark etched lines of tree trunk
after tree trunk, a language of the forest, telling the story of what lived
and died there, evergreen trees unflinching to seasonal change. winter sweeps
over the scene like a foreigner, dancing as she turns, her
ivory skeletal hand caressing flower after flower, as they wilt
into her fingertips. it's easy to look at her and say destroyer, but really
she's just an avenue of change, a spellcaster, like anything in
the woods that moves, winter dances, but you don't know the tune.
hurricane heart-rate as ink pools in, an evening, desolate, silent, eerie,
what was once bright is absent, echoes that sound like questions, an absence
of understanding, an abundance of possibility. bury me in the creek,
as the shallow water dances over my body like a trapeze, the stars poke needle pricks
into the canopy, and dare to tear waxing holes of light through
the layer of trees and night air. soon they are spotlights, soon this is a crime scene,
soon you are screaming, and the forest whispers back in its own language something
you could never receive, the dusty skyline speaks like a traveller, she knows the earth,
and the way to make it move, and you, you are but the riverbed,
and the bones of fishes from times b.c. to last week, a medley of dead things,
and yet screaming life—how to be a calamity, something that grabs a tree and shakes it
by the roots, you speak back to the skyline, and she says, i am eternal, but you
are you

CLAIRE
Lucy McEleney

Shovel in hand, reputation in the other.
A botched job lies, encased in slander.
I find you on your hands and knees in the graveyard,
digging up the worst of us—
two girls with twin tombs and matching bouquets
finding ways to reanimate old pain,
zapping life back into old wounds
and burrowing into each other's brains.

You looked for a place to plant the bones
so that you could watch the conspiracy grow,
vines creeping up through the cracks in our stones
and gasping up through the mess of rumours below
until you can't read our last name.
You won't find our mother here,
but we can keep pretending just the same.
I'm scared she would be disappointed.

I can be such a foul little thing,
sharp as the needle-point bones of my elbows.
Car-seat squabbles and cider bottles
have gathered in piles on the kitchen floor—
now we're constantly tripping over the past.
Hot-stinging tears and open-mouthed howls
are the background noise to my adult life,
and I still have the headaches from 7am starts.

We could still paint over your dirt-caked nails
with varnish I got in old magazines,
I promise I'll never tell a soul
if you promise we'll never have to form teams.
I'll keep choking down crematorium dust
and put on my best display of trust,
covering up the thick coat of rust
as we try to wipe this chapter out,
like I don't still carry it with me.

I'd never tell you, but in my dreams, we're still speaking;
the way we used to, when you'd sneak into my room.
I tell you how I hate people looking at me,

that I can't open my mouth in case they see
what everyone else does now—
I fuck everything. I've fucked my own destruction,
but I could never cower behind such a deception.

I was there when you learned to ride a bike
and I'll be there when your body falls apart in a public bathroom.
I was there when you needed someone to blame
and I'll be there when you run out of people altogether,
but there's nothing I can do that would make this better.
We are moulded and muddled the same.

TUSCAN SUN
Maddy Hadwin Donnelly

My face is wet, my thighs are wet, I'm slipping on the toilet seat, trickles of gin running down my legs, the cuts and grazes where I fell. My vagina is sopping, stinging like I cut it into ribbons then used the ribbons to fry chillies. I slam my fist against my face and sob into it. A glass of straight gin lies smashed on the floor. When sobbing becomes ridiculous, my fist falls, I notice West Brom —fucking neighbours naming their fucking cat after a football team—staring at me through the open window with its quivering eyes. 'Leave me alone,' I scream, wrenching the toilet roll off the holder to chuck at the cat. 'Leave me fucking be!' It hits the windowsill. The cat treads lightly onto the laundry basket. 'Don't you dare…' It sniffs at my pants, where I left them, their contents stained and runny like egg yolk, its tongue in small, darting motions, begins to lick. 'Don't you fucking dare!' I make to rush at it, forgetting my jeans around my ankles—the floor turns to soap, flies up and smashes my nose open—

The sun comes up when I open my eyes, pokes at my corneas. West Brom is sleeping peacefully on my chest, his tail looping around my neck. The pressure feels like a hug. Last night's grief comes to mind like I watched it in a film a long time ago. I remember hitting my head, blood, bathroom tile. Clutching at the cat like it could fix me. People say don't drink alone; then living alone is damning, or—worse—self-punishing.

Blake messaged last night—*When can I see you again? Xx*

Never. *You gave me a fucking sti*

He replies immediately—*You have an sti? god if you've given it to me I swear—*

I fire back *You piece of shit*

He calls me a *Whore*

I don't reply, another message pings through—*So when can I see you again?*

I sit up, vaguely aware of West Brom's protests as he lands hissing on the carpet, before slinking away. A few empty bottles are scattered across the floor. Two days ago, Mum told me to 'get it together, Mia'. I felt like she'd torn something off me, and when I left it would lie there on her living room carpet and before long it would wither and disappear and I'd never get it back.

My vagina itches like hell. Reaching a hand down my pyjama bottoms, I feel something wet, and make a scooping motion. When my hand comes out it's covered in a yellowy gloop, tinting my skin, getting underneath my fingernails. For a long time, I stare at the colour, raise my fingers to my nose and sniff.

'Does it smell?'

'Yeah—I mean—a bit. A bit fishy.'

The receptionist doesn't make any notes, her manicured hand still on the mouse, leaning forward and asking curiously, 'What colour?'

'Tuscan Sun.' I'd held up my fingers against my computer screen, the colour chart. Like the meditation tapes say, I looked with total curiosity. Browsed paint shades online.

'And does the area hurt?'

'It mostly itches, and there's some pain.' I hesitate. 'More since I poured gin into it.'

She looks at me like I'm not all there. Gin does not burn out your problems. Not even a little bit. 'Why did you do that?' she asks, shaping her words like, *are you okay?*

'Um.' I try to smile and shrug my shoulders. 'You know.' I let out a fake laugh, it sounds like a cough. 'I just felt like it, I suppose.'

We pass three consultation rooms with female doctors, but I'm being seen by a Steve Buscemi lookalike. I had a dream where Steve Buscemi was a priest who sought me out and shot me for not attending mass; now I can't watch *Monsters Inc* without experiencing a flood of religious mortification. Watching him typing on his keyboard, I shift uneasily in my seat. He wants to know what's wrong, and I wonder if the receptionist asks on the off chance it's something freaky, an anecdote to share, a plea for thirty seconds of undivided attention.

I can't say the words Tuscan Sun. 'My discharge is yellow,' I tell the Doctor. *Go on, Mia.* 'Like Tuscan Sun.' He raises his eyebrows—Buscemi's there, gun raised, *ave*—but doesn't comment. There are a few more questions, he tests my sample using a coloured stick, then hands me a prescription.

'Take these twice daily for ten days.' As I'm leaving, he adds, 'Ms Chalk?'

'Mia.'

'I don't mean to judge, to pry in any way... but I am a GP.' As if it's a *Blessed rather are those who hear the word of God* scenario. For a moment it's like he's finished, and I'm standing there, foolishly, as if I can't bear to go. 'We advise no alcohol with the antibiotics,' he tells me, his words full of nudging significance. 'I wonder if you might like a leaflet.'

I don't glance at the slip of paper he's holding out to me; I know the like — *long term problems of alcoholism... cancer is on its way over with a crowbar, don't hand it your address.* 'I'm okay. Thank you.'

'Ms Chalk—'

'I'm okay. Thank you.'

Crossing the road at the junction, there's an instinct to fold into the stabbing pain in my uterus, but I keep walking. Reaching for my phone, I go to safari, and it opens on paint samples.

As the colour disappears from my knickers, it appears on the walls of my home. With each brush I deposit myself in the world, paint over the words of everybody I want to leave behind. The pain lessens, I feel healthier, I get paid and buy succulents. Bottles go under the sink to make room on the windowsill. West Brom comes in from the balcony and I show him around because everything feels new, he sniffs the wet paint and sneezes, departs with dyed whiskers. The doctor emails me a link to a support service and I block Blake's number after he sends me photos of his dick, a video of him wanking.

'I love the colour,' Mum says when she facetimes. 'What gave you the idea?'

I have enough paint left for anything she might say, so I admit, 'I had an STI and my discharge was the colour of Tuscan Sun.'

'Ah.' Her face takes on its familiar clouded look, 'Mia…' and in those two syllables something in me droops — I forgot how she can make me hurt so easily, I'm thinking *why, why*—and I'm in danger of being like I was before.

'Mum… don't.'

I cannot, I will not, lose this feeling. There's something brilliant in being surrounded by the contents of my vagina.

FROG
Magda de Soissons-Page

Frost-tipped toes pointed in awe at the open morning.
I am eight, maybe nine,
and a little frog has frozen in the night.

His little belly swollen with the cold air
is taut like a green grape and I tap it
just to see.
It trembles underneath my Barry M pink nails,
bitten to the quick.

Surrounded by sharp grass and red-wine mud
frozen in small peaks
he looks out of place.
I take him inside to warm up
and give him a tupperware pond.

He just floats, toes now curling over in disappointment at my ceiling.
It is not the fresh sky he was admiring amongst his preserved peaks.

I think oh, no. I am too late
and I go and bury him
right under the gate.

GENESIS, TODAY
Maya Elphick

Is this worship
to watch you,
warm and kneaded by sleep,
drifting off in the sighs of sunlight
through the sash window
in, in and then out again,
making roots in something dark?
Eyelashes dancing on the dewy tears of yawning,
like black geese on the lake
whipping water up into gathered hems of blue lace.
It will be time to wake up soon,
to stretch our legs and our arms,
to carry the bulb in the palm
and plant it.
To kneel in the morning's dirt
and pray.

THE YELLOW ROOM
Megan Dennison

She made her way, room by room, seeing it all for the first time. The old tenants' unfinished projects and corners left bare. What the place could have been before they packed it up. She picked up a box in the hallway—"Misc. shit" scrawled on the front in permanent marker, brown tape ripped loose from the lid. Things shuffled around inside, and the corners hit the walls with each climb up the staircase.

Soph?

Yeah?

Are you coming to say goodbye?

I'm just checking everything's here. I'll be out in a minute.

The steps annoyed her again with their steep decline, and she thought how easily they could make her fall. How she probably would, in a rush, one day. She made it to the bottom, safe this time, and carried on through the hallway. Switched off the light and left the door on the latch behind her.

Think that's all of it.

Her mum, stepdad and brother all looked in her direction.

Great. I think we should probably head off now, darling. Before it gets dark. Anything else you need before we go?

That's okay, I think I should be all good now.

She left them with hugs.

Thank you for everything. I'll call you tomorrow?

And send us photos once you're all set up. Make sure you eat something, too. Yeah?

She thought about the empty fridge.

Will do.

She stood by the gate, watching them clamber into the car. She waited until they pulled into the road, lowered the windows to wave, and made their way around the corner. Listened to the tyres cracking along the concrete as they moved further into the distance.

Until they were gone.

The first night was cold. Sophie fiddled with the thermostat, desperate to find a patch of warmth. Fumbled through boxes, looking for a pan, a spoon, a bowl. Something to cook. A can of soup, the one she'd usually avoided, left somewhere in the back of a cupboard. She struggled with the stove, then the fuse box. Lost patience. Gave up. The can found its regular spot on a new shelf. She piled a duvet, blankets—all of them—onto the mattress lying on the floorboards. She pushed it against a wall, away from the draught, and curled into the covers, her unfed tummy rumbling. Gathering the duvet between her freezing toes, she tucked it under her feet. Morning found her in the same spot, phone dead. Door still on the latch.

Every room was an unreturned deposit in its own right. After endless email exchanges with the letting agents about the state the place had been left in, she ran out of legal phrases to steal from Google and gave up fighting. Her mum came equipped with spray-bottled chemicals, J cloths and scourers on moving day, and had raised her well enough to know how to use them. Her portable speaker boomed on a constant loop, filling the quiet house with the country songs she'd cleaned to with her mum and sister, their voices matching each other's pitch with ease. She drowned out the empty house now with her singing, lungs filled with bleach fumes. And even though she knew the words by heart, she couldn't quite find the harmony.

The doorbell rang, and she turned the music down. She arrived to the slamming of a heavy piece of mail—a catalogue of some sort, or a magazine subscription not yet redirected—on the doormat. Most likely never to be claimed, along with the other letters left behind.

She picked it up, slid her thumb underneath the seal and pulled out the magazine. She walked with it into the living room. Its white cover read, 'Design Anthology,' embossed on the thick, matte paper, followed by subheadings: 'Interiors,' 'Art,' 'Architecture,' 'Travel,' 'Style.' Issue 07. A woman on the front, scooped up by a black barrel armchair. Teacup pressed to her lips, golden light cast across her face. Sophie pictured the woman in the room with her, nestled by the fireplace, green tea steam rising.

No woman actually looks like that. Peaceful.

Sophie brought the envelope back to the top of the pile, flipping it over to see the name on the front. She wanted to put a face to it and reached into her memory to find one. But nothing came to mind. Just a name on a white envelope. She grabbed her laptop from the coffee table and opened it, screen lighting up her cluttered desktop. Google. Facebook. Her cursor ran to the search bar. 'Mia Sands.' Nothing. 'Mia Sands, Cambridge.' She clicked on the first profile. Mum of seven, which a two-bed house would never accommodate. Second profile, two mutual friends. Some woman from Cambridge—the Massachusetts one. She leant her head on her hand, digging her nails into the nape of her neck, and scrolled on. Tenth on the list. One mutual friend, some guy from her old job. She flicked through the profile photos. One selfie of wild curly hair after another. Of arms slung over shoulders, faces pressed together. Of opened books in hands. Sandy coastal beaches and walks in the woods. Each frame was captioned with anecdotes or one-liners. Sophie continued down the profile, to the photo albums. She flicked through them, every part of this stranger's life on show. Every moment, captured. Baby photos, a newborn girl. A hand wrapped around a finger. First steps. First birthday. First words. Rainy walks, tiny boots jumping in puddles. Another birthday, another candle lit. Sleepy cuddles. The same white crib in the same little room. The one upstairs, with the window looking onto the garden. The wallpaper, yellow with daisies.

Sophie wandered upstairs, laptop still in hand, to check out the beige box room, now stripped of all joy. She knelt by the doorway and inspected the cover up — picking at the bottom of the cream wallpaper with her fingernails, right at the edge of the skirting, until a corner came loose. There they were: the daisies. She moved to the other side of the room and lifted up some more. What started as an urge to pick became a desire to pull, tearing off a full strip and revealing the pattern beneath. The stripe of yellow across the wall rebelled against the room. Begging to be seen. She worked her way around, frantically ripping some more. Bits of the old came off with the new, but it was mostly intact. She kept going, arms aching more with each tug, until there was none left uncovered. Piles of paper thrown across the floor.

* * *

A home had become a house. Scuffs on the walls from the backs of chairs, now revealed. Imprints from flat-pack furniture still marked in the carpets. Blu tack stains from every memory stuck down. Patched up holes from each nail in the wall the landlord said not to make again, in the rooms he said not to paint. Ghost pictures, shadows where they used to hang. Their perfect outlines above the fireplace, where the soot settled. The place was empty, but it was all still there.

Someone else's life, in pieces.

Mia Sands' Facebook profile was bookmarked on Sophie's browser. She returned to it daily and worked her way through every album of Mia's life—past to present. 'Stella's 1st Birthday.' 'Writers' Retreat.' 'Halloween Party '20,' her latest fixation. Every angle of the house could be seen through the stills of drunk thirty-somethings in fancy dress. Draculas, cowboys, Greek goddesses, all throwing themselves at each other and drinking from plastic cups. Mia sipped from a water bottle in the corner, her little bump dressed like a gumball machine.

Sophie analysed each pumpkin bunting-framed scene and hunted out the same white IKEA bookshelves, mid-century coffee table and wooden dining set. A near-identical rattan crib for the yellow room. She bought as much as her overdraft would allow and isolated herself for two weeks, rebuilding the home in the early hours and sleeping in the afternoons. She kept track of time by the various delivery notifications buzzing on her phone, her front door opening onto a new set of strangers with big parcels each morning.

The doorbell went again, but it was her best friend, Gina, standing there this time, with a bag of snacks and wine bottles clinking at her side.

Sorry, I should've messaged first, shouldn't I?

Gina stumbled in, shoes shuffling across the mat and bringing the shock of winter in with her. Sophie pulled her hair up into a bun, trying to mask the six days she'd gone without washing it.

Don't be silly.

I've just been dying to see your new place, and we're both so crap at organising anything. Thought you might still need a hand getting some shelves up, or something? Or at least someone to get drunk and giggle with while you do it.

She pulled out a bottle and held it up in the air.

It's ten in the morning, Gi.

So what, it's five somewhere, right?
I've missed you.
I've missed you too, my love. Come on then, give me the grand tour.

Sophie hadn't quite thought about explaining the yellow room to people. The baby's room, sitting empty in a single woman's house. She tried to avoid it as she showed Gina upstairs, tiptoeing around the shut door.
Is this the spare room? For when I have a life crisis?
Gina gripped the doorknob as she spoke. It was impossible to have any privacy around someone so transparent. And then she was in the room, eyes instantly locking onto the crib sitting by the window.
Jesus, Soph. Is there something you want to tell me?
She burst out laughing, turning to look at Sophie standing nervously on the landing.
It must look so weird, I know. I'm not pregnant or anything, don't worry.
I just wasn't expecting *to see that*. What do you need a crib for? Think it's a bit small for me, though I am flattered.
Sophie returned some forced laughter.
The old tenants left it here. The landlord said they left in a rush—moved overseas, I think—so they couldn't take everything with them. Thought I may as well keep it, you know?
So, you promise that's all? It's totally normal if you're still grieving, Soph, but this might make you feel worse about it.
It's not that, honest. But you're right, I'll put it in the loft tomorrow.

* * *

The yellow room started filling up. A pine chest of drawers full of little socks and nappies and bibs. The closet held baby grows, little vests and knitted jumpers on a row of hangers. Everything with the tags taken off and fixed permanently in their space. Sophie kept the room warm, letting in the sunlight each morning, and drinking her tea by its window at golden hour. She maintained a routine of brushing off any dust that had settled and refolding the blanket in the crib at every opportunity. Before she left this time, she pulled a baby scan out of her pocket, along with a pregnancy test, both blue lines fading but still just about visible. She placed them into the crib—tucked them in—before making her way out and locking the door behind her.
The rest of the house had been restored to its previous state, as close to it as possible. The sofa wasn't quite the right shade of grey, and she didn't have enough photos printed to fill an entire wall. Her dinner table was set for three, though she was the only one. The same set of cutlery ended up back in the sink to be washed up for another day. The same plate. The same silence. The place was all made up, a home without a family. There was no baby sleeping soundly in the crib, no books to be read. No songs. No words to be said to anyone. Just some rooms in a house, ready to be taken.

THE WORLD ENDS
Mia Galanti

The world ends. Ashton moves south.

Her parents have a house in Northumberland, so when county borders first start closing she gets in her car and drives down. *The pathogen is transmitted through bodily fluid*, the radio says on the way up, so she changes stations until it's playing some country song filled with twinkling banjos and yawning violins, and turns it up as loud as it can go. She's brought a potted plant for company, her Nancy Drew box set for entertainment and two jars of peanut butter for sustenance. A box of condoms, too. They did say bodily fluid, after all.

The gardener is dead on the couch in the living room when she arrives, skin grey, eyes open and milky-white. She closes them with a pair of rubber gloves, then goes to the shed for the wheelbarrow.

She supposes she'll have to get used to this.

*

Ashton doesn't know which of her parents turned first. It could have been either, maybe her dad shared a drink with someone whose skin was beginning to go grey beneath the collar, maybe her mum was a little too dismissive to a server who spat in her food five minutes before his eyes clouded over and he went for the fry cook. One of them must have brought it home, kissed the other on the mouth, slipped in some tongue because he'd brought back dinner or she was wearing her nice red dress.

It's not like it mattered, anyway. By morning they'd both gone grey. Ashton locked them in their room and sat outside holding a knife, mouth filled with blood and eyes with saltwater, listening as they forgot her name, and then each other's, and then their own.

It was around midday when they finally fell quiet.

Grief's a weird thing when it's coming in droves. Ashton went out to the back yard to bury them and found her next door neighbour already there with a shovel, stone-faced, a body next to him. He was looking down so he didn't see her, but she saw him, and the grey veins crawling out from the ends of his shirtsleeves.

She ended up dragging them to the ocean. She prised off their wedding rings, rolled them off the end of the dock into the water, and was back in the car before they hit the seabed.

Her tears tasted of saltwater.

*

It's quiet, up here.

There's no one around for miles, just endless bogs and rolling hills. Ashton likes the quiet for the first five days, and then on the sixth starts seeing moving shadows in her peripheral, hearing voices whenever she opens cupboards or sits too long in one place, so from thereon out keeps the television on whenever she can. It's only a matter of time until the signal cuts out, anyway.

On the seventh she unearths the wine cellar, which smells of mothballs and is dusted in a fine, filmy layer of dust. The only bottles left are the expensive ones, with sleek minimalist labels and near-black glass, or necks warped into clever shapes like perfume bottles. Ashton was never much of a recreational drinker before, but she experimentally uncorks one anyway.

The smell of fermented grapes that hits her nose is almost identical to the stench of rubbing alcohol she'd used to get the stains of her parents out the floorboards. She barely manages to cram the cork back in before she's dry heaving on the floor.

She doesn't go back in there again.

It's a little lonely. But it's also the end of the world. So she's not sure what she was expecting.

*

On the fourteenth day, she gets visitors: Chris Knight, from high school, who went by his full name and sat behind her in Geography, and another blond boy she doesn't recognise. Chris has grown a lot since school, which is the last time she saw him: taller and broader, skin like toffee in the sun, hair bleached almost as fair as his friend's. They're both the same colour as the scrubgrass when they come to the porch of the house, bare shoulders bright in the sun.

Chris introduces his friend as Peter and explains that they're just passing through, but Ashton offers for them to stay longer, because the house is too big for one person in the middle of nowhere. He's sweetened, Chris, since high school, grown into his ears and shoulders, his smile soft on her over the dinner table as they eat (chickpeas from a can, tomatoes from the garden, grown fat and sweet and splitting).

"It's just me, now," she says, when he asks about her parents, and he reaches over to touch her hand.

"I'm sorry," he says, looking her in the eyes. His hand is warm.

On his other side, Peter is watching them out of the corner of his dark blue eyes with a sharp, canny look. He hasn't touched his plate, just sits back in his chair not saying anything, repeatedly poking his finger with a needle. He catches Ashton trying to catch a glimpse of Chris's wrists as he gesticulates, and slowly, sarcastically, turns his own out.

His veins are green, not grey.

She can't help but feel disappointed. By the way his gaze hovers heavily on her, even long after she has broken eye contact, she thinks he might just be able to tell.

*

The heating had stopped working on the ninth day, along with the electricity, so that night they all huddle in the living room, piled beneath blankets and pillows. Chris is in the middle, and Ashton watches the expanse of his shoulders, until, on his other side, Peter's breaths even out. Then carefully, slowly, Chris turns, until they're facing each other.

"Is this okay?" he whispers.

She nods.

It's good. She thinks that maybe it's because the last time she touched someone it was her parents' cold skin as she rolled them into the ocean, or maybe because the giggles about Chris Knight's fingers in high school were all true. Whatever it is, it's nice, and it's good, and he's sweet, and when afterwards, he kisses her, he tastes of the overripe tomatoes.

"Thank you," he says.

She closes her eyes so she doesn't cry; when Chris's breaths even out, she opens them again. In the reflection of the television, she can see that Peter is still awake, poking his finger with the needle, over and over.

*

"You should come with us," Chris says, one day. "When we leave."

When has become nebulous; it's been a while now since Chris and Peter arrived. Ashton knows their leaving is trickling closer, like a ticking bomb. Boys like Chris Knight, like Peter, are made for movement, they'd never be happy remaining passive and still in an empty echoey house, where the cupboards whisper and the silence has grown claws. The house has become a little less empty and echoey with them around, like it has grown to accommodate them. Like it's at rest when it's filled with laughter.

"I can't," Ashton says.

"Can't, or won't?" he counters. Ashton doesn't know how to respond, until from the doorway Peter says, "Ashton?"

"Coming," she says.

The garden is bright and overgrown, smelling sweetly of rotten vegetables and damp soil. Peter is showing her how to grow tomatoes; she'd asked, and he'd said yes, though she's not sure why either of them made those choices, because they're not friends. Chris is really the only thing they have in common: bright, colourful Chris, who is probably the only reason the house has seen warmth at all. Ashton tries not to be jealous of the way the house has formed around him the way it never did with her; now more than ever she feels like a ghost in it, unable to compare to him and his *aliveness*.

At least Peter feels a little ghostly too. Like neither of them quite have enough life in them to ever match Chris.

"I get it, by the way," Peter says, finally, and she looks up. It's the first time he's instigated conversation; usually they sit here in silence.

"Get what?"

"Why you can't come."

She presses down on the soil with the tips of her fingers. "You wouldn't want me there."

"No," he says. "But that's not why you're not coming."

The sun overhead feels very hot, all of a sudden. She wants to pull off her shirt, but she's not sure how Peter would react. She still thinks, sometimes, of his blue eyes in the darkness of the room that first night. They've never talked about it.

"No," she says, finally.

Peter waits.

"It's lonely here," she says. "But it's… a place." Not home. Not yet. Probably not ever. But… "It's stable. Peaceful."

She'd be lonely, but rather lonely than afraid.

"You haven't asked him to stay," Peter says.

"No."

He could never settle down here, for one. And secondly—

"Do you think you're a good person?" she asks.

She's unsurprised when he says, "Not really." There's a pause. "You?"

"Me either."

"Yeah," he says.

There's not really much else to say.

*

The night before they're set to leave, Ashton makes the bed in the master bedroom. Peter walks by as she does so, and for a moment their gazes meet in the doorway.

Then he keeps walking.

It's good this time as well, maybe better, because they know each other's bodies now. Chris is unfailingly gentle. He holds her hand, pushes her sweaty hair off her forehead, makes eye contact the entire time. Ashton kind of wants to cry the whole time.

Afterwards, as they're lying on the bed, sweaty and satiated, he says, "I love you."

She keeps her eyes closed and pretends to be asleep.

Later, when she hears his breaths even behind her, an arm tucked snugly around her waist, her back against his chest, she takes his hand, laces their fingers together. Turns his wrist. She's grieved, but not wholly unsurprised, to find that his veins have gone grey.

At least she had the condom.

*

She thinks of that neighbour, digging a hole in the backyard, half-turned.

She wonders who he was digging the grave for.

*

Chris dies sometime in the afternoon. She doesn't know when. Peter helped her push a bookcase against the door of the bedroom, then pricked both their fingers to make sure they weren't infected, too. Then she went to the garden so the buzzing cicadas would drown out the sound of his screaming. She's there for so long that her shoulders tighten, her neck grows slick with sweat.

Peter joins her a couple of hours later. His face is expressionless.

"Is he…?" Ashton says.

Peter nods.

She puts her chin on her knees. They watch as a bee lands on one of the flowers. It's the first bee Ashton has seen the entire time. It's funny, what nature can do in the absence of human intervention.

She doesn't like to think that Chris dying helps the bees.

"I don't suppose you're planning on sticking around now," he says.

"No," she says. "Probably not."

They glance at each other. In the direct sunlight, his eyes are a different kind of blue, clear saltwater, like the ocean she left behind, that's wrapping around her parents.

"There's a shit-ton of expensive wine downstairs," she finds herself saying.

Peter smiles, maybe for the first time.

It's day eighty-one. Ashton's parents' faces are beginning to get a little blurry in her memory, so she takes the bottle with the warped neck, and doesn't say anything when Peter takes two bottles with minimalist labels. They pile them into backpacks—Ashton takes Chris's, soft around the shoulders, smelling of grass and sweat and Chris—and then they load a paper bag with their tomatoes. "So we can plant them later," Peter says. Her face must do something because he straightens, almost strangely self-conscious; says, "What?"

"Nothing," Ashton says. "Let's go."

She realises, later, that she was smiling.

CONVENIENCE
Mica Magsanoc

The cheap bells will chime, and the lights will sting
Your muddy shoes will tread on the newly polished ground—
no worries, I'll clean it up later
The shelves make mazes, the freezers mean dead ends, the people deciding
between fruity or minty sweets are roadblocks
Walk past the sodium-packed chips, sugar bombs on sticks, the shimmer
of newly packaged cookies, and the smell of 3-month-old pastries
Head for the machine in the far back corner; but the red light will flash—OUT OF ORDER
Take no for an answer
And bang your clammy hands against the cool metal and rock it back and forth without pity
The red light will flicker out and the machine will hesitantly start whirring
Now wait—four taps of the foot, two shakes of the head, one click of the tongue
Grab a flimsy red cup and stick it under the spout
The lever will feel the comfort of your hand, and the cool, blue liquid will spill out
Layer by layer the cup will get filled; grip it tighter
When you release your hand, the lever will feel the absence of you
Pick up your cup and walk away
Past the stocked shelves, the undecided, and the person calling out for payment
And out the door that chimes with remorse
That's what you do best.

ALL SAINT'S EVE
Ollie Briggs

Every year on the eve of All Saints' Day, as the light faded and threw long shadows across the hills, and the sun bled and burnt past the horizon, Godric would be forced to hobble into the village and recite to a rapt audience the tales of his youth. At first, Godric had smarmily wallowed in the townsfolk's awe at his part in capturing the Citadel of Acre and loosening Saladin's grip on the Middle East, but age tends to bring with it grumpiness, and Godric already had that in spades.

The first time anyone had ever questioned him about what he had seen, Godric had leaned back on his seat and exhaled dramatically. What had he seen? He was tempted to reply with some stoic grunt that implied terrible, terrible things: *"Nothing good."* Part of him wanted to tell the truth: *"I saw my friends shit themselves and die from sepsis."* That wouldn't do either. For one thing, it was a great honour to have served under Richard, and besides, the asker of the question was no older than eight, far too young to be burdened with the images of soldiers bleeding out in their own faeces. He had eventually opted for a middle ground. "Everything I saw," Godric had said slowly, putting his hand on the young lad's shoulder. "I wish to leave in the past."

Godric sometimes wondered what he'd do if he ever ran into the young man on All Saints' Eve. He imagined the boy standing up amidst the crowd, shouting out, *"If you want to move on from it so badly why'd you show up here every year and go on about it?"* Godric certainly wouldn't have an answer for that. Perhaps he'd—

"Alright, mate?" Godric was uncomfortably wrenched from his musings by a figure who appeared as if by magic at his side.

"Heading to Dunkeswell for your—for your talk?" Edmund was clearly out of breath but masked this by patronisingly slowing down and matching Godric's lopsided gait. Godric tried to stop himself from groaning. He rather enjoyed the peace and quiet one gets on a walk through the country, and a surprise visit from Edmund was pretty much the best possible thing to shatter that calm. Every village had its wizened veteran with a story to tell. Most villages also had an idiot.

"Guess what I'm doing," said Edmund, continuing before Godric had a chance to even consider any possibilities. "I'm running."

No bloody need to rub it in, thought Godric as he raised his eyebrows in a display of mock interest.

"Ah," said Godric, nodding and smiling. He paused. "…Why?"

Edmund had obviously been waiting for Godric to ask this.

"It's apparently *really* good for you," Edmund said. "It helps your heart, it helps your humours…keeps you fit! Siegfried told me, he's getting everyone in Dunkeswell running all over the place." Edmund clapped his hands together. "You're headed there, int'ya?"

Godric nodded and spoke wearily. "Off to tell my tales." Edmund grinned.

"'Course you are. Best part of the autumn, for my money."

They walked in silence for a few paces. Something in Godric stirred at Edmund's words. He almost felt proud, but he had to remind himself he was not proud of his time in the East. Part of him wanted to tell the village that, rather than the same three stories about the siege of Acre, watching prisoners getting decapitated, and the time he saw a lion. But the villages liked those stories, and Godric almost liked the village, so for the past thirty years he had been willing to compromise.

Further down the road, Edmund spotted a gaggle of men he knew headed for the village, and jogged down the lane towards them. The birds in the trees sang as they would at the break of dawn, and Godric wondered if they knew the difference between the sunrise and the sunset.

The stars were peeking out of the sky when Godric arrived in the village. The campfires were lit in a clearing surrounded by the village's rustic dwellings, a communal area where the townsfolk were out in their droves tonight. Godric reckoned the last time he had seen this many people was exactly a year earlier, the last time he had come to speak. There was the familiar stage, with a wooden lectern that had probably been pilfered from the church, just for tonight.

Godric never thought to practice his stories. Even when he first started telling them, the memories were fresh enough that he could just pull up an experience on command, embellishing it slightly each time or making minor adjustments for the audience. Was the crowd in good spirits? Something patriotic and bloody. Were they drunk? Don't get political. Few too many kids? Leave out the bits about vomit and shit. The odd parent would sometimes get in Godric's face and demand an explanation for why he had elected to tell such an inappropriate story, and in his younger and slightly more volatile years, Godric would have thrown back a snide remark. *Why're you taking your kid to a talk about the bloody Crusades then?* Or, *I'm just saying what I saw. Maybe just shit happens,* if he was feeling particularly entitled.

Godric was now older than most of the village lot. That definitely had something to do with why he got less concerned parents. It got him free mead, too, but tonight he decided to wait until after he'd spoken before getting slightly pissed.

Edmund's words earlier had, embarrassingly, stuck with Godric. Taking his familiar spot on the stage and glancing out at the clusters of people, he saw Edmund and some of his mates give him a wave, smacking someone's shoulder and making them spill their drink. Godric smiled half-heartedly, and once the jostle had died down, he leant forward and clasped the sides of the lectern. Seeing the anticipation that writhed through the crowd was damning.

Tonight, Godric had wanted to be honest. To tell the crowd that the Third Crusade was nothing but a fool's errand to the desert under a disillusioned King. He wanted to explain how he could not look at a plate of meat, or a cow-skin throw, or a fleece jacket without thinking about the living soul that had died for it, for he had watched men die for less. But the earnest anticipation in the crowd stopped Godric short. He knew what everyone wanted, and what he wanted most of all was for the evening to wrap itself up with little departure from the annual routine.

So, when Godric began to talk of valiant soldiers and heroic sword fights, he felt himself slip into the sense of comfort that comes from avoiding the path less travelled. Any notion that he was doing his fellow man a disservice by being dishonest about his time in the East was overtaken by the sense of victory he felt in his gut as the crowd roared and laughed exactly when he wanted them to. Louder and harder than any other year, too.

A recluse by nature and his own admission, Godric missed out on the celebrations on All Saints' Eve, electing instead to leave after a drink and a round of collecting praise from the village folk. He missed out on learning that Siegfried was looking to volunteer more men for the Fourth Eastern Campaign. Perhaps there was nothing he could say that would stop them. Perhaps he did not care. As long as men went East, there would be men like Godric who returned empty, and men like Edmund, who would not return at all.

ISOLDE
Paloma Parás Ochoa

Time has the power to transform what was set in stone in the past into something as malleable as the clay that was moulded by the artist. At least those were her thoughts as she turned the car down into the lane, unaccustomed to the perspective afforded to her by the front seat. She was able to remember how much she had dreaded those monthly visits. The long drive up, the heat, the myriad of insects. Cat Stevens playing in the car, courtesy of her dad, while she muffled the noise with her headphones, blasting whichever obscure rock band she'd discovered and fallen in love with that month.

Switch on summer from a slot machine…Oh I know we've come a long way…

Now, looking at the place through her newly wrinkled eyes, she didn't understand her past self. Those days in the countryside without access to the Internet had prompted her sister and herself to be active, both in mind and body. They had given her a lifelong friend. Back in the city, it was easy for her to fall into the role of the untouchable older sibling, dishing out small morsels of kindness when she felt like it and retreating into her own world the rest of the time. The countryside was different. It was impossible for her to ignore her sister because there was nothing else around. And it had been precisely in those isolated days that she realised she actually liked her.

She decided to park the car some way off in order to walk down the stony and uneven road. As soon as she got out, she could see their past selves sprinting down the stones in front of her, memory invoked in an instant by the aromatic smell of the bougainvillaea flowers that resembled a Monet painting in the way they added clumps of pink and purple to the path. They had raced up and down that path, making up stories and chasing each other, her always in the lead while her sister's shorter legs pumped hectically in an effort to keep up. Those nights when they would go to bed and their bodies immediately relaxed, as if they had spent all day swimming in the sea and were just now letting loose. That satisfying feeling of being active and using their muscles, as opposed to just sitting in a chair for hours.

The wind picked up and brought her back to the present. The breeze that caressed her bald head was the same breeze that had tousled her bangs as a child, and will be the same breeze that plays with the leaves in the tree that would outlive her.

That tree. They had named it Sprout. She didn't quite recall…Oh! It had all started with the sign they found propped against it, "Brussel sprouts." Some leftovers of a harvest long dead. Sprout rose above all the other trees, colossal in his old age, big enough that the branches acted as comfortable resting places and the leaves rendered the people walking by blind to the girls' presence.

She rounded the corner and walked up to it, placing her palm flat against its scarred surface. She closed her eyes and a smile tempted her lips. Her sister had always been the kooky one. Even her name had a magical ring to it: Isolde. Ice Queen. Mythical princess. Sister.

She used to squeeze shut her eyes and scrunch her nose, small hand on a tree trunk.

"Not again, Isolde…" Both plea and complaint.

"Shhh. I'm communing with Sprout." Fingers on lips.

"Oh yeah? What's he saying then?" Exasperated sigh.

"He's telling me secrets…Saying that…"

What? What was he telling you? What secrets did he hold? What did the leaves whisper, what did the bark groan? Why was it that your soul spoke to living things like that, where did that connection come from? Is nature wise? Does it know…

She opened her eyes and moved her palm away. Something must have hurt the tree because the pads of her fingers came away sticky with resin. She knew better than to try and wipe it anywhere, things would just stick to her now, like bees to honey.

Glancing up, she considered climbing the tree, but knew her body lacked the litheness that once held her hand. It would be no good anyway. She had lost the ability to wander the castle of her imagination long ago. She glanced at Sprout one last time. The sky had darkened, the tree lacked the leaves it showed off during the summer and seemed to her as ancient as the stories of knights and dragons her mum had read to them when they were young.

Looking to her left, past the car park, she could make out a much younger tree. Taller than her, bigger since her last visit a few years ago. But still young. It felt as fresh as yesterday. Green.

It took her a while to walk over. A combination of the dizziness that suddenly invaded her and the fact that each step brought her closer to the memory of that day.

The day that was supposed to be just another star in the constellation of her life, but now felt like a black hole in her memory.

She was able to recall every detail. The weight of the purple mug in her hand, the chip it had on the handle from that time she had dropped it. Running her tongue over the roof of her mouth, the tea had been too hot, she had burned it. The call, the sudden nervous laughter that bubbled in her chest, her body's automatic reaction to the news her mind was not able to immediately digest. The emptiness. The weight that had settled into her shoulders and around her neck, a weight that had never quite vanished, despite the years. The only person she longed to call, the only person rendered unavailable by an unlucky case of time and place.

And this new tree that she now stood in front of, an invitation to remember, to live, to rejoice. A gateway to the past and those two eyes that pierced hers, depthless, holding secrets she would never get to know.

She made herself look at it, not just staring but actually focusing and registering every single detail. The young leaves that still clung to it, refusing to fall in the cold of winter. The bark, unmarked by the years to come, strong and sturdy but still so thin when she compared it to the other, older trees.

As if directed by some outside force, she put her palm against it, closing her eyes as her fingers came in contact with the wood.

"Where do we go when we die?" Isolde's soft voice, questions. Still believing that her older sister held all the answers.

"What? What would I know about that? I'm still here, aren't I?" Pause. "And even so, I don't think we go anywhere. It's just a long rest. Inky black forever."

"I don't agree." Palm against Sprout. Eyes closed. Slightly smiling.

"Oh, please tell me then. You, who knows all about it." Exasperated. Waiting.

"I'm not pretending I know anything or everything. I just know what it feels like when I put my hand against this tree and I get some kind of energy. I don't know, it makes me think. Maybe we're not so different in the end. Maybe..."

Maybe? Maybe you were right. I want you to be, you know? I don't think I believe it but that doesn't mean I wouldn't like to. To believe that someone who was once so intrinsic to the world has not been lost to it. To believe.

She moved her palm some ways down, almost as if she were caressing the tree. Infinitely gentle, infinitely searching. With her eyes closed, her sense of touch elevated, the pads of her fingertips transmitting details that her brain would have otherwise missed. Her hands followed an invisible path down the smooth surface. If it hadn't been a while since her last visit, she would have thought they were acting on muscle memory.

Finally, her fingers traced the words that were carved just as neatly in her heart. Isolde.

CASCADE
Robbie Tyler

I
I saw an internet-armed generation reaching for the Stars! to pick out the rapists and deviants,
  Souring the limelight, jeering, pointing at stray pubes stuck to public apologies, leaving a well-dressed Movie Monster to hump the wall of a cell for 23 years, refusing oil to the machinery of
  a Hollywood night, of star-studded darkness, who chipped Moloch's veiny horn, whose talk would glint awkwardly with the gold-toothed language of advertisement, ventriloquized by the unchippable Gucci gold hand of Moloch,
  who'd google, with pixel-pregnant eyes, in the bar where thoughts might have gathered, argued, and multiplied like formless sexual entities,
  for whom cashflow groans in the plumbing of their Dreams,
  whose thoroughbred weeds could upheave pavements and family trees, making the young
  old and the old young and a rhino fucking dizzy,
  who wasted their radiant cool gaze on soldierboyman games, shooting up,
  whose cocks limped into early retirement from too long in the warm flicker of manufactured
  sex dreams, where pixel-fleshed apparitions manifest with intravenous efficacy,
  who knighted the divergent professor with eggs, saw blue legs goose stepping over hard electric
  people, and so shot at them with cameras,
  who saw statues kneeling on necks, and dragged a colonial with sparking ankles, and cast his
  metal in the doc, then rolled and smoked up a police van for passing notes to Teacher,
  who bombed tesco with rhythmic missiles of verse til security apologised, and ejected them
  from the cereal aisle and the applauding, defrosted customers.

II
I saw a generation who truanted in the crumples of West Country, across a patchwork blanket of farms and woodland, wearing sleeping bags and the cider smiles of frilled ancestors, telling firelit tales of buried rap, tales of dragons, roaching chemistry books and bewildering Bats with bassy air (those scatty little angels will never fly straight), who looped sound, rhyming stutters at line-stunted open mics, in lung-stain basements, in the undergrow of Hotwells hip hop, in
  oblique, rainbow rotted Houses with Alice-pilled interiors,
  Houses busted for squatting under the Suspension Bridge like city skulkers, haunted with
  colourful, too-friendly ghosts and the insatiable skeletons missing their charming rock,

Houses with supernatural glazing, teeming with the dilated pupils of an exceedingly high school,
pupils cramming, impossibly, for the test of the abyss,
who made love in a duvet nest, on a hill, on a farm, in a tent, in a lightning storm, in the death—
dance of solipsism, where souls raised blind touched for the first time, gasped, touched again, reading skin's braille as heads buried and the lightning's flash flooded the love with light, thundering its two cents to which the tent, the freckle sized fire defying the sleety, screaming
universe gave rapturous reply,
who were spared by an ostensible, smoking black stump on a neighbouring hill from a 300000000 volt orgasm of death, and in the morning were confronted by a frowning flock of
residents, all storm-draggled wool and wordless; armed with a blunt syllable,
who returned that eve and spiked a sheep to which it stared at the same spot of sky for days without sleep, a cock-eyed devil, playing goat, a zero-yard stare, boring into heaven's obsidian tissue and starry sinews, letting out an abrupt bleat when it spotted God; a gargantuan terror,
headed, toothed, eyes empty and indifferent, looking at worlds as a bear looks at snowfall,
who breathed two-litre coke bottles of fog, dashed Names on molecules like first son skulls on a tizoc stone, tasting Otherly wine (overflown bodies with notes of razor wire), peeling three eyes to spot Machine Elves, peeling off prefrontal clothes to dip and drown in the pearlescent
Bathhouse of a communal dream,
who woke on a carpet stain to find their Egos had waited up for them with tapping feet:
Deathless as cartoon characters, pissed as pissed mothers,
who woke and confused a pine-silhouetted Sunrise for a nuclear explosion, dropped in embrace, shrieking as hilarity exploded from Fear's cocoon, before mundane realisation dusked on that dear second forever.

III

I saw an optimistic architect, twisted in the rubble of her illusion, laughing in a hard-hat, twisted,
I saw an opportunistic Builder getting smaller and smaller, vanishing into the sky, into the
rarefied cocaine air about their monolith's ever-growing, ever-headless neck,
I saw a pessimistic critic, trodden into the duvets, sipping sweet coffees and curling his I-told-you-sos, baring the invisible, meridian shaped scars of childhood abuse,
I saw one murderous incel and a million unwitting associates, treading the forum threaded
bridge further and further away from a cardboard cut-out of Humanity,
who leered up at a Couple on the balcony, doing laundry, rolling out their bed

sheets like a
   coat of arms on a castle, drying each other's blood in the sun: victorious,
   I saw ill minds look in the mirror with contempt, as they cut their bodies open, a pragmatic
   surgery, an auto-vivisection to remove the father,
   But it can't be done, he's in deep with the 10001010111011010010111000100s of the soul and
   the reset's a sexless figure of tooth, chewed by a pillow of maggots,
   who looked in the mirror and tried to wrench off their glasses, stained like a church's and fast
   to their heads, visions imprisoned in off-rainbow dysphoria,
   who looked cool though, pretending not to hear the world, themselves, that symphony of
   creaks and groans and snaps, that symphony of breaking; growing.

BIRTHDAY PT. 2
Rowena Price

Meeting the flat slate of a new face
I find I am sickened by the last
long strain of you. The cubicle bowl
meets holy material; outside the bar
the sky tastes of me and she takes me
home. Make no mistake, I would not
purge what needs not purging.
This makes grown meat of me, keening
out the infant underbelly: the memory of
the softness of your hands. This keeping
my own to myself these days.
This pushing through folds of stale air,
tearing the breach a fresh vernix
of curses, lone & naked
& woman on the other side.

SOMETIME, ILLUMINATION
Rowena Price

Tonight I leave the curtains undrawn
while you emboss your breath on glass
and *show me where your favourite freckle is.*
Together we make shapes with sound, skein
our bodies out under sunlight.
I see the weight of your head
in negative on my pillow—
warp and weft in my palms, offering
myself for the uncoiling, loving
the heft of your absence.
Two atoms strike
The wilful beam of air.
Tomorrow I will open the window
on somewhere to sit with the trees
and watch your hands do the talking for you.

TOY HORSE
Seb Lloyd

I watch while copper Witches miss their hour
to oxidise shadows the other Children sleep
walk within a dance alive with night
mares in the mirror of equine eyeballs
Moonlight pebbledashes across the outhouses
catching the other Children's
mother-of-pearly skin refracting ash of blue
that carpets the eyes of the yearlings
Stabled late on the turn
of the solstice

In the place of the fire where I
burned
Copper Witches usually rust the gates
awaken the stables
Our wooden horses taught the foals
playfulness in a state of
paralysis
Obstinance in a state of
Horror
Paralysed and rocking within stalls of smoke
Dressage for a Wraiths waltz
ashen boys on
cinder foals

The rockers remain
in the courtyard
bodies of toys I played with
when I first read Animal Farm
In the courtyard where pigs addressed the square with authority
like crows at traffic lights
the other Children try to forget my cremation
Collect my memory between their toes
A marker of the shadow cast on their souls

Horses are the only animals to need shoes
In the ruin
Fulfilling my vow at the turn
of an hour my last solstice the shoes
were all that remained

Stripped of skin
and screaming as one
smelting the body of a boy and a foal
I terrified the witches away
For one hour a year on the turn
I know how to hide from
Nuckelavee;[1] from the shades
of the ruins
I watch the turn
Of the solstice

---

[1] The Nuckelavee is a hybrid creature from Orcadian mythology that combines human and equine features. It is skinless, and was said to have had black blood.

BACK TO US
Sophie Wallwin

INT. AVA'S HOUSE - LIVING ROOM - NIGHT

The scruffy but warmly lit living room of a student house, a group of 5 getting ready to leave. The carpet is threadbare, two worn out couches line perpendicular walls, and there is a hollowed out fireplace opposite. There are photos and bad drawings scattered around the walls. The scene is littered with the remnants of an evening socialising, empty bottles, a pack of cards spread across the floor.

There is minor chaos as everyone (JOSIE, KATIE, LUCAS, WILL) locates coats/wallets and finishes drinks. AVA, 23, is standing by the door in the corner and ready to go, wearing a loud,80's style jumper and a short, bluntly cut bob. She has a slightly vacant expression, seemingly disengaged from the scene around her.

INT. JACK'S HOUSE - BEDROOM - NIGHT

Small bedroom, also clearly a student house. There is a small patch of mould on the ceiling, a laptop open on someone's Facebook page and a suitcase still not fully unpacked. The room is dark, lit only by a lamp. There is a sink and mirror in the corner. JACK, 22, is brushing his teeth and rummaging through his wardrobe. His hair is dark and overgrown, he is slim, medium height, and wears a faded t-shirt with a woven bracelet on his wrist.

            MADDIE (O.S)
(shouting from downstairs)
   Jack, are you ready? We're off!

            JACK
(through a mouthful of toothpaste)
   Coming!

He pulls a jacket out of the wardrobe, spits toothpaste into the sink and rinses his mouth, then glances up at the mirror. He lingers for a second, eyes locked with his own reflection, expression blank.

EXT. STREET - NIGHT

Jack, HARRY and MADDIE walking briskly down a street of terraced houses, cars lined up either side. Harry is dressed scruffily, with baggy jeans and a knitted hat. Maddie is tall, the same height as the boys, with blonde hair in two buns and a purposeful walk.

It's not yet late, but the street isn't busy. The three are all pulling their coats tighter around them, hands in pockets and breath visible. Harry gives Jack a sideways look.

                    HARRY
This'll be the first time you've seen her, won't it?

Jack nods, not looking at his friend, face unreadable.

                    MADDIE
We don't have to stay the whole night, you know. If it gets weird.

Jack considers, then shakes his head.

                    JACK
It won't. We're fine.

EXT. PUB BEER GARDEN - NIGHT

The small, busy, covered beer garden of a pub, full of groups of young people. It is dark, lit by the warm light of string lights above. There is a group at a table, drinks already in front of them. They sit, wrapped in coats and scarves.

Ava is squashed on a bench seat between Josie and Will, who have clearly been engaged in heated discussion. Katie and Lucas are sitting opposite.

JOSIE
Will, all I'm saying is we shouldn't sympathise with people like that. It's enabling.

WILL
I'm not sympathising, I just think you're being close minded. Having money doesn't automatically make someone a bad person, everyone fucks up -

LUCAS
So, we should give a free pass to anyone who can afford it?

WILL
That's obviously not what I'm saying -

Ava has a bored expression. She has clearly heard these debates before.

AVA
You three are so great for casual pub chat.

KATIE
I don't know, I actually love spending my Friday nights debating the classism of social justice.

As Katie is speaking, Jack, Harry and Maddie enter from the street outside, glancing around. They spot the others and grin, walking to join them at the table. Jack is the last of the three. Everyone exchanges greetings.

HARRY
Alright! You lot look cosy. Do we need a couple more chairs?

He locates two chairs from a nearby table, giving one to Jack, who seems distracted.

AVA
Harry! What do you reckon, is it time for a dismantling of the bourgeoisie?

                    HARRY
          You know my opinion mate -

He pulls his chair into the table, sitting down as the
others look at him. He looks mock-seriously into each
of their faces, speaking slowly and deliberately.

                    HARRY (CONT'D)
          Eat the rich.

Everyone laughs, letting go of the conversation.
Jack has pulled up a chair at the end of the table.

                    MADDIE
          Drink, anyone? Jack?

                    JACK
          I'll go. You get the next one. Pint?

INT. PUB BAR - NIGHT

Jack is leaning on the shabby bar, which has the same
air of friendly dilapidation as Ava's house, putting
his wallet away and waiting for the drinks. Ava en-
ters through the door behind him. She stands next to
him at the bar. Neither of them look at each other.

                    AVA
          Hiya.

                    JACK
          Hey.

                    AVA
          How're you?

                    JACK
          I'm alright. Tons of uni work but yeah, I'm fine.

                    AVA
          Good.

She looks around, clearly grasping to find a topic of neutral conversation.

> AVA (CONT'D.)
> Did you get that essay back? That you were doing before?

> JACK
> Oh, yeah. I did alright.

Jack considers.

> JACK (CONT'D.)
> Did you get your car sorted?

> AVA
> Not yet.

Three pints are placed in front OF Jack. He quickly picks them up and turns to leave.

> JACK
> See you back outside, then.

> AVA
> See you.

Jack is walking towards the door, pints in hand. Ava has a pained expression.

> AVA (CONT'D)
> Jack!

He turns around. For the first time in the evening, they look at each other directly.

FLASHBACK
INT. AVA'S HOUSE - LIVING ROOM - NIGHT

The living room is busy, there are people sitting on every available surface, even more standing. It is warmly lit and everyone has drinks in hand. Ava and Jack are sitting on the sofa, squished in between strangers.

We can't hear their conversation, but they are close, touching legs, arms, and talking easily. Jack says something and Ava (unsuccessfully) pretends to look offended, then breaks into laughter.

Jack gets up to fetch another drink. Josie comes over to Ava, asking her a question. Ava nods in reply, only half listening, as she watches Jack go into the kitchen, a smile on her face.

BACK TO PRESENT
INT. BAR OF PUB - NIGHT

Ava and Jack are still standing, gazes fixed on each other.

              AVA
I - I just thought - I want it to be normal, you know.

              JACK
(beat)
Me too.

She is looking down, fiddling with her purse.

              AVA
I don't know how to - to do it.

              JACK
I know. I hate this.

They stand in silence for a second, looking at each other still, words stuck.

Jack exhales a half-hearted laugh, shaking his head, and turns to leave.

EXT. PUB BEER GARDEN - NIGHT

It is later in the evening, drinking well and truly underway, the atmosphere lighter. The group has split off into their own conversations, laughing and talking over each other.

Jack finishes his drink and stands, extracting himself from the packed table. Maddie watches him.

> JACK
>
> I'm going for a smoke. Anyone?

> MADDIE
>
> No, you enjoy it mate. Make sure you suck up all that lovely tar.

> JACK
>
> (Rolling his eyes)
> Nice.

EXT. STREET OUTSIDE PUB - NIGHT

The street is lit by the orange glow of a street light. Jack is standing, back to the wall and facing the street, rummaging through his pockets, lighter in one hand. Ava appears from around the corner.

They are clearly both a little drunk and in better spirits, the coolness of before thawed by good friends and alcohol.

> AVA
>
> There you are!

Jack smiles as he sees her, holding out one arm as he pulls a pack of cigarettes out of his pocket with the other. She leans into it, familiarly. Jack breaks away and leans against the wall, lighting a cigarette and looking at her teasingly.

> JACK
>
> Looking for me?

Ava laughs.

> AVA
>
> Suppose I must be…just wanted to see you, I guess.

Jack suppresses a smile.

JACK
I get it. I am fucking irresistible.

Ava laughs again and takes the cigarette from him.

AVA
Glad to know you haven't changed. Ego just as big as ever.

JACK
You've never been able to fault my consistency.

AVA
Now THAT is true.

Ava smoking, Jack gives her a sideways look.

JACK
You had me worried earlier, at the bar. Thought we'd have to do the whole 'bitter, awkward exes' thing.

Ava gives him back the cigarette.

AVA
Fuck, I know. Can we not do that, please?

Jack looks at her with mock seriousness.

JACK
On second thoughts, I don't know…you did let me down pretty hard…

Ava gives him a shove, he bats her away, laughing now.

AVA
Don't do that. Come on, back to the others.

She goes ahead, back around the corner to the beer garden.

AVA (O.S)
(calling back to him)
Don't want anyone getting any wrong ideas!

Jack hangs back, smiling. He stubs out his cigarette, composes himself, then follows her.

EXT. STREET - NIGHT

The group (excluding Jack, Harry and Maddie) are walking in the glow of orange streetlights. The others are ahead, calling out to each other, laughing as Ava straggles behind, her face rosy and cheerful. Someone calls her, she laughs and speeds up.

EXT. A DIFFERENT STREET - NIGHT

Jack, Harry and Maddie are walking home. Harry and Maddie are talking, Jack is in his own world. He smiles to himself, shaking his head slightly.

ONE MILLION NERVES
Synne Solbrekken

Because I lick them when I'm nervous
Because I don't want cold sores
Because they get thinner as we age
Because they tingle after contact with spicy foods
Because the colour is caused by visible blood capillaries under the skin
Because I use them when I speak
Because I want soft kisses
Because they have a cupid's bow
Because they have the thinnest layer of skin on the body
Because they let me smile
Because they are unique like fingerprints
Because they have over one million nerve endings
and they'll tell you when I'm nervous

UNDER THE ARTIST'S LOVING EYE
Thomas Smith

They recently had a new door fitted. One with green and yellow panes where the panels once would've been. Walking up to it, you put your feet firmly together, looking down at your tightly drawn laces. Everyone inside knew you'd be late, so much so they could've betted on it.

After knocking, a distorted image emerges through the window in the door advanced. Knowing who it was, you smiled briefly to yourself. Opening the door slightly, his face pressing against the frame, he says, 'You made it then', proceeding to open the door fully.

'Happy birthday, Calum,' you say, stepping into the house, 'am I on time?'.

'When have you ever been bothered by that?' Calum says, guiding you through to the kitchen. Upon entering, everyone was turning their heads to look at you, as if you are a stranger. Some were smiling, some returning to their conversations. Conversations about you. As if being there didn't fill you with anxiety. Jenny, however, (Calum's wife) came bouncing over to you with a flute of prosecco in her left hand, showing off her wedding ring.

'Anya, I'm so glad you could make it', she says, with a slight viciousness to her tone, bruising you with her eyes. She hated your presence. Seeing you as a threat to her marriage, always knowing that Calum loved you more than her. But moments pass, and you missed yours with him.

'I'm glad too, I've bought a present', you say, taking the rectangular shaped gift out of your handbag, passing it to her.

'Oh, that *is* generous, thank you', she says, placing it on the island, 'you're lucky you came now, we were just about to sit down to eat'.

'Well isn't that lucky'. Jenny grinning, began to collate the guests, calling them over to sit down for dinner. While passing you, Calum placed his hand on your waist. You felt him again. A feeling of wanting that you craved. It felt dangerous, but he continued to the table, not looking back at you. But you knew. It was a sentiment through touch.

As everyone was sitting down, you made sure you sat the furthest away from Calum. You didn't even want to throw a suggestive look his way . The thought of giving him anxiety on his birthday wasn't high on your list, so much so, you weren't going to turn up at all, but you knew it would be rude if you didn't.

Jenny began tapping the side of her glass to get everyone's attention, while catching Calum's quick glance at you.

'Ok, speeches', she says, 'now, you know I hate giving them but today is about Calum. It's his special day and I'm so happy we can all be here to celebrate it together. To Calum', everyone raises their glasses, chanting, 'To Calum!'.

After the starter, you were hiding in the toilet, to have a breather. You were noticing, at the table, people sharing looks between each other, as if they were making presumptions about what happened to you. Out of your bag, you began to pull out a letter, addressed to you, from Calum, from three months ago. He always wrote such beautiful letters. It read:

Dear Anya,
You always lived an interesting and yet somehow completely normal life and I'm sorry if I mistook normality as stability. I always remember you keeping old bus tickets at the bottom of your bag, which I always found strange but I now know why you did that. It was a reminder of who you were, what you've done, where you've been. A linchpin, from then and now. But I think that's what's killing you, forever keeping one foot in the past. If you keep holding onto them, it's as if you're standing at broken traffic lights. Waiting for the green man to come, when ultimately you know they won't. So please, for me, eh, take that leap of faith. And I'm always with you. C x

It was a relationship that never really ended with a dramatic break up but ended on a quiet Tuesday night, and, in that moment, where your lives seemed so far apart, you thought the best thing to do was end it. But it was your biggest regret. And when you received that letter, it was in a moment of emptiness. It was the day you came back from hospital, after your overdose. You were so lonely and tired of not being loved or wanted. You thought no one was there for you but he always was. Yet, you thought, the painful impossibility was that love just sometimes isn't enough to save someone and you'll fall apart either way.

After the main course, you were standing outside, in the garden, having a cigarette. Calum was behind you, peering his head out of the French doors.
'I thought you'd be here', he says.
'Well, you did watch me leave,' you reply. He was slowly moving towards you, in a perfect, peaceful silence. 'Think about it, if you stayed with me, you might not be boasting about getting a new front door,' you say.
'No, I would be boasting about my incredible, artistic, wife and then try and make people jealous over our *marvellously decorated walls*'.
You started laughing at that, knowing perhaps you have at least one thing over Jenny.
'Why did you do it?' he asks, as you were dropping the cigarette to the floor and stepping on it.
'Do what?'.
'You know'. He pauses. You placed your hands deep in your pockets.
'Because, sometimes, everything hurts a bit too much. And I was sick, and I couldn't bear it. I couldn't bear it any longer'.
'I wish I could've prevented it'.
'You did, this time. If I'm honest you're the only reason I'm still here'.
He looks at you kindly with misting eyes.

His presence, momentarily, made you think about a couple of weeks ago, when it was raining heavily and you weren't expecting anyone, just a quiet night in.

Suddenly, however, there was a banging at your door, with Calum's voice arising from the outside, 'can I come in?'.

Running to the door, you let him in, pushing hard on the jammed handle.

'What are you doing here?' you say, closing the door behind him.

Before answering, he completely froze, staring at all your portraits hung up and around in this somewhat small flat.

'I thought I'd come to see you,' he says, still distracted by the paintings.

'You're soaked through. Do you want me to call a taxi?' you say, walking towards the bathroom to find a towel while he was still enamoured by the range of art before him.

'No, do you mind if I stay here tonight?' he says, taking the towel off you, rubbing it through his hair.

'Why?' you say, watching as the rain dripped off his face, onto his shoes.

'I just …' he says, pausing, thinking about his next words. 'I just want to be with you, right now'. You stood slightly below him, your hand reaching up, wiping away the rain off his face.

'It's like you're crying,' you say.

'Like?' he says.

After a moment of you looking deeply into his eyes, and him reciprocating, you nodded.

'You can stay on the sofa,' you say, 'I'll find you another towel, then send an invoice'.

'I'll reply with a kindly written letter,' he says.

Walking away from him in the living room, back into the bathroom, there was a feeling. One that felt like it should be alien but in fact it was simply dormant. You felt love.

Later, when you were sitting with him, watching tv, turning to you, he asks, 'can you draw me?'.

'I can yeah.'

'So, will you?'

Looking away, you were thinking of the lines you'd make, how you'd pose him, and the colours you'd use. You suddenly realised, you didn't even need him there to draw him. Yet, as a model, you were always interested in using him. But morally you found it uncomfortable. However, here was an excuse.

So, standing above him as he sat on the sofa, you began undressing him, peeling back the oversized t-shirt you found at the bottom of your cupboard. Combing his hair, running the brush through every dried knot. Stroking his eyebrows, to straighten them out. And then you began. Using a small sketchbook, you were positioning him in many poses. Using different lighting. Casting shadows. Making tons of small studies and bigger studies. In charcoal, pencil, ink.

As you were drawing, you felt he could read your mind. You are two people who can't live without each other, but the agony that you can't be together, creates art. Him listening to your most intimate thoughts, and you drawing them.

By the time the morning came, the rain had stopped. The sun bled through the existing hanging paintings, showing the textured lines of oil paints like road maps. And like that, Henry left, with his now dry clothes, and a moment of intimacy fulfilled. And you looked through the sketches, picking out the best ones. The ones that would be best to paint. Turning the pages, with your charcoaled fingers.

Back at Calum's birthday party, everyone was beginning to leave. The meal was over, drinks had been drunk, speeches and small talk had reached their conclusions. You sat in the corner the whole night. Not saying anything really. But thinking. Thinking how much you'd give to sit at the front of the table and give that speech. Thinking about how much you wanted Calum. When you lost everything and you felt like the last thing to lose was your mind. You were wrong. Calum was always the last thing to lose. As you got better, he wasn't there to watch when you wanted him to be. Even in the moments you were drawing his eyes, his lips, his nose, you thought, yes, this is right. This is where he should be. You and me.

Sitting in the garden with him, you thought, you should be mine. When he touched your waist, it wasn't one of sexual tension, no matter how much it felt like it. It was one of honesty, and for the first time in a long time, you didn't feel lonely and that he might still love you. So, as you were leaving, standing in the doorway which led from the kitchen to the hallway, turning your head to look at him, you were hoping he'd look at you too. But he was picking up glasses and did not reciprocate a look. Not even a glance. So walking away was the only answer. But as you were leaving, he was watching. A sense of longing filling him. Because he was looking, and so were you, but those looks were missed. And in those looks an impossibility was solved, but for no one's witnessing eye. The dream of him telling everyone about your marvellously decorated walls was slowly fading away but he could still picture it. You and him, walking into gates of eternity. There was no better conclusion.

Once it was all over and Jenny was going up to bed, he was looking through the presents. Most of them were superficial, like funny mugs. Upon finding your present, its book like shape caused intrigue. Just sitting there, neatly wrapped in brown paper. Opening it, he found a sketchbook. Full of the drawings and studies of him. Flicking through the pages, he caught himself smiling, as their beauty touched him. Not *his* beauty, the delicate, intricate skill.

Your work gave him peace, it gave him hope in you. Because if *love* still breathes, there will always be hope.

At the end of the sketchbook, sat a folded-up piece of paper. Unfolding it, placing it on the kitchen table, in its A2 glory, presented an oil painting of one of the sketches you'd done of him. And sat next to him, also in oiled brilliance, was you. *Always you.*

THE OTHER SIDE OF THE LAKE
Tianyu Zhou

If a thing moves, it creates beauty.
When sitting beside you by the lake that Sunday morning, Joe, I finally realised what it meant.

The water flowed in front of us. Its movement was hard to notice. Some fallen leaves were floating on its surface. They were all being carried in the same direction, having no choice but to follow their own fate. But you didn't see any of this, Joe, for you were reading, with your head down like a withered flower. You turned the pages with your thumb and forefinger, hesitantly, not willing to let go of the parts you already finished. Then, the page moved, and so did your fingers.

I was also moving. Sitting there with only a light jacket on, I shivered just a little. A soft breeze blew towards us, the water flowed quicker. I could hear my own heart beating. A moment later, I blushed, and covered my cheek with both of my hands, pretending I was just cold, not nervous.

Suddenly, you looked up with a frown, and stared at what's in front of you for quite a while. I tried to look in the same direction, but couldn't turn my eyes away from you.

"What makes a leaf fall?" You asked, having no idea that I loved you.

"That's just what happens when the season changes, I guess."

And then, you were lost in thought again, like you always were. How bad I wished the time could stop.

"Its dryness, maybe." I said, "When a leaf dies, it becomes dry, and that's how it loses its connection with the tree branch."

After hearing what I said, you stood up, and threw your book into the lake. We watched it float on the surface for a few seconds, before slowly sinking into the water.

I was shocked. Did I say something wrong? I thought to myself, and seeing you, Joe, being so tall beside me, for I was still sitting; and looking calm as the surface of the lake.

"Joe, come back," I said when you began to walk away, but you didn't seem to hear me. "Come back." I raised my voice a little, but it was no use.

So I just sat there, puzzled, watching your legs move back and forth, and back and forth, until they carried your body out of my sight. And that's how easy it was for you to leave me, Joe. I felt so overwhelmed that even my body stopped shivering.

We are both moving. We always have been. You had chosen to move in your own way, and so did I. But whenever I think of you, Joe, I'll think of the lake, I'll blame myself for not standing up to walk with you. I'll close my eyes and be taken back to the very same place you left me.

It was a cold Sunday morning in late autumn. Leaves were falling from the trees. I was sitting by your side. You were reading. A soft breeze blew towards us. You looked up from the book, with a frown and a look in your eyes that I can still recall even though many years have gone by.

What exactly did you see?

You leaned your head against the windowpane, breathing heavily, lips slightly parted, as if words were going to come out at any second. But you wouldn't let them, would you, Joe? For you had always been so calm and reserved, never said a thing without a second thought. I wanted to remind you of the view outside, of how rare it was for the sunlight to shed on those trees this early in the morning, but your eyes looked so numb that I doubted you even cared to look at it at all.

Apart from the driver, we were the only passengers on this bus. I sat on the seat beside you, which means if I wanted to look out the window, Joe, I'd have to look at you. I liked sitting beside you, even if I'd be further away from the view, and to feel the touch of our knees when the roads were bumpy. While the bus was moving as a large rectangular box, I felt like my whole world was trapped in it and was moving along with it.

"Joe, I think the bus is going in the opposite direction."

"Don't worry," you said, "it goes in circles."

When you said the word "circle", your voice clearly shook. You're feeling carsick again. Both of your hands had already clenched into fists.

Your breathing became faint as the bus was taking us closer to the lake, which made me think that you must have fallen asleep and were wandering in some far-off places within your own head. All of a sudden, I felt close to you, and found it hard to ignore the tension between our bodies, except that yours was unconscious. I wanted to laugh like a little child and run in my old princess dress towards where you were. I'd be faster than the bus. I'd be faster than anything in this world. People would think I was mad, they would even be scared of me. "I'm not mad." I would say to them, "I'm running towards my love."

A sense of numbness began to spread in my arms and stopped them from moving. I felt as if you were holding my hand. But when I looked down, both of your hands were still in firm fists. If it wasn't your hand, Joe, then what was it?

I hadn't realised how heavy my hands were until I tried to put one of them on yours, just like several weeks ago.

"Tell them!" I remember you saying, almost beginning to yell, after I told you I was scared to go back to my homeroom, because those girls could always find a way to lock me in, "Tell them what you feel and it's not okay to treat you like this!"

"But I'm scared, and it'll be no use."

"Why are you scared of telling people what you feel?" Your tears were coming out, though I couldn't tell if it's out of rage or sadness.

"I'm sorry." I put my hands on yours to calm you down, "I'm really sorry."

You eventually decided to skip all your classes and sat beside me on a bench until school ended. We talked about so many things that I actually believed would come true one day, when you're still by my side.

The edge of the lake appeared in my sight while I was recalling. I had to wipe off my tears before waking you up for the bus stop.

"Everything happens for a reason." You said to me as we walked along the lake, "The water ripples for a reason."

As years kept passing by, I got to learn that the most powerful things were the ones unseen, and that I'd be in great pain if I failed to notice them. This uncertainty in life scared me. Sometimes, I could even see it coming to me in my dreams, and I would wake up screaming. But wasn't it the most intriguing part of being alive, Joe? Wasn't it what drove all the living things to move and create beauty?

"Maybe someone's drowning on the other side." You followed up. Was that why you believed the water would move?

I was out of breath at your words. And while you kept on talking about some random things that happened in school, Joe, the sky shook above me.

It became rather clear that something's standing between us, splitting us apart. You sat down next to me when we're getting a bit tired, opening up a book which I didn't remember the name of. I tried to overlook this sadness and felt the urge to let out my feelings. But you have to understand it wasn't easy, Joe, for me to find the exact words that I clearly knew would put our friendship at risk.

So I watched the willows gently sway in the breeze as their leaves fell. Beside me, you were reading. The pages were turned after a long time of hesitation. When those things squashed into my sight all at once, I felt giddy with a sudden shock that pierced through my body.

I could see it, Joe, I could see the beauty in their state of being, and how those invisible matter flowed underneath, driving them to move. This is the moment, I remember myself thinking, my feelings deserve to rest at where they belong. But when I turned my head and saw how your eyes were still fixed on that book with its printing small as black dots, Joe, my courage vanished like a flash.

A few seconds had passed, and you looked up with a frown. You saw the death of those leaves while I was appreciating their beauty.

"What makes a leaf fall?" You asked.

"Its dryness." I answered.

Then, you left me, Joe, with your legs moving back and forth, easy as how a leaf fell from the tree. That was the last time I saw you. I recall myself remaining seated by the lake until the moon rose, and rushed back home with the tendency to fall down onto the muddy ground. Later, when I looked into the mirror, I could no longer recognise my own face.

I burst into tears with the vision of us jumping into the lake together. The water was so cold that we had to paddle fast enough to keep ourselves warm. Unlike those leaves, we could swim in whichever direction we wanted. I'd follow you all the way up to the other side of the lake where you once thought someone's drowning. I'd hold on to you as tight as a leaf did to the tree branch in early spring. And when it was about time, I might even be able to tell you how much I loved you. The water would then be moving because of us, because of the tension between our bodies that once pulled us far away from the rest of the world.

Joe, I really miss you. I later heard you moved to Europe and were happily married with kids. Sometimes when I was once again wide awake at night, I blamed myself for letting you go.

But if I were to stop your legs from moving, Joe, if I were to stop the water from carrying those dead leaves all in the same direction, the world would lose its beauty.

Right now, I need to stop thinking. What had happened cannot be changed, just like how we used to sit in the same position but could always see different things. I close my eyes and for the last time see you walking away from me, towards the other side of the lake. How beautiful. How cruel.

Not until this moment do I begin to see, that what was standing between us all this time, Joe, has never been the lake, but its movement.

A MATTER OF PERSPECTIVE
Victoria Her

All my life I had always seen the bad things as inevitable, and the good as waiting to turn bad. So, it came with some surprise to find myself as God of an unknown realm. What do you do when you become God, you might ask? Is it all it's cracked up to be? I could answer all that, but all things have their beginnings, and this is mine. It's my story and I'll tell it in as long-winded a manner as I like.

Everything started at home. Home: a place of refuge, respite and occasionally a leavening agent to madness. I lived by myself. Four walls with their peeling lines and wet patches. Small indents hiding blobs of paint, though I sometimes thought it might be dead insects stuck inside the walls. I remember that I burnt my tongue on my tea, and it had gotten swollen, but I couldn't stop staring at the ceiling. You kind of disappear for a moment into a world of quickened breaths, heartbeats, and shaky limbs. There *had* to be a flood upstairs. The ceiling looked wetter than the day before, so the logical conclusion to be drawn was that it would come crashing down on me. I couldn't ask the neighbours if there was a flood. What if I looked insane? And I definitely couldn't call… Who would I have called? The police? The fire brigade? And I certainly couldn't search up who to call. What if that looked suspicious? And if I looked suspicious then I definitely would never be able to get a job. And if I never got a job then I'd be homeless, and oh my God. I'm going to die. I clutched my chest. My eyes felt like two dangling entities, separate yet connected to me by a thread. A very delicate thread that was very close to snapping. Shit. My palms felt unrecognisable. Their sheeny glean like the ceiling. Clothes too tight. Walls too small. Shaking and blurry. The thread could snap at any moment. My eyes darted to the ceiling. It couldn't snap. It couldn't. And that's when it happened. It snapped, and I became God.

The world shattered into mosaic pieces. But as each piece fell, as the walls dropped giving life to the outside world, as the outside world gave way to the sky, everything came together. From the remnants of the past, I found myself in a field, on top of a floating rock. And that's not a figure of speech; I was literally out of this world. A jagged rock, with a hue of iridescence at its core. Humming with life, mechanical connections driving the rock forward towards the purple syrup sea. That's when it struck me, my first clue. From all the way up here, how did I know what it looked like down there?

A rustle, and my eyes flitted to meet the perpetrator. Grabbing a fist full of the powdered diamond soil, I felt my voice waver. "I've got a weapon, so I'd be careful if I were you." The rise of my chest came into view. Eyes stinging. I was going to do it. Turn around. And. And what? I spun around wildly. The thrown powdered diamond soil dissipating through the wind into the startling cosmos all around me.

There. Right in front of me. A birch tree. Its eyes. Real. One was bloodshot, and the other was blinking, a startling blue. I saw one green eye glaring. A black eye felt like it was smiling. Looking at everything around me. Nothing was strange. It could have been beautiful even. All I was thinking in that moment, how creepy, and I wished that the eyes would go away.

So they did.

I blinked. The birch tree seemed perfectly ordinary. I touched it, feeling the roughness of each indent. An uneasiness clawing at my neck. Tentatively, I looked behind me. A patch of the glinting soil displaced. So, at least that was real. Had I imagined the tree? At that moment I suddenly had enough of it all. To be in bed, under my covers clutching my fuzzy hot water bottle, a cup of tea just in reach. I closed my eyes. My fluffy socks warmed from the radiator, the gentle thrum of cars an anchor point. I opened my eyes, and just like that, my vertical world became horizontal. Falling out of the stratosphere and into a place that looked like the bedroom I had always dreamed of. That was the purpleheart wooden wardrobe from the antique store! A giddiness rose in my chest. It would be great if there was a chocolate fountain. I glanced instinctively to the left. Chocolate fountain. I let out a laugh that I didn't know had been compressed in my stomach. Marshmallows, I thought. Then I realised that I was really not thinking big here. World peace? No, no. That was too vague. Did people even exist in this world? Wait. Was I on Earth? Or was this that other realm, the one with the syrup sea and all-seeing trees. I popped a chocolate-coated marshmallow in my mouth. The sickly sweetness hugging my insides. The more I chewed, the stickier it got. What if it sealed my mouth shut? My eyes widened. A rush of heat swept to my face. My mouth. I struggled. Reaching for the tea and scalding the corners of my lips. Help. Shit. Is this the afterlife? I always thought Hell would trick you into thinking it was Heaven. That's always seemed the cruellest to me. People say alternate worlds exist and that we couldn't possibly be in the worst timeline. But wouldn't the worse one be one in which you thought that somewhere else is worse off? Because the worst one would be comforting. Knowing that you're experiencing the worst means it can only get better.

That's all I needed; a moment of distraction. I really do want to eat the marshmallow, I thought. I swallowed, and that's when I realised. They must do personality tests for deities. How on Earth did I pass?

So quick re-cap, I found out I had become God, and I did what someone might do. We're getting to the in-between bits and I'll skip ahead. You know, I always thought complete control was what I wanted. I thought life would be easier if you knew everything that would happen to you. But then again, bad things are inevitable and the good waits to turn bad.

I travelled the world at least three times over. I went to all my favourite worlds that I had seen in film and video games. Oh, side note, most of them are absolutely terrifying. I went to space for a few years, or it may have just been a couple days. Mars is not what it's cracked up to be. Hard to tell time these days. I went back to my version of Earth. Put in place communes. Removed corruption. There was no more hunger. Food was sustainable. Everyone worked to their ability, and had free time to pursue leisure activities and hobbies. Tried my hand at painting, then gardening. Well, I did everything I'd always wanted to. Knew everything that would happen. Let people get on with themselves for a bit. No wars. Nothing. Absolutely nothing. So why did I feel the gnawing feeling that something was wrong?

It patted my shoulder when I first travelled to Mars. Flicked my head when I visited Scotland. Gave my legs a kick when I painted. That's when things began to change. Limbs more conceptual than real. Over time I thought that someone could read my thoughts. Maybe there was another deity that had it out for me. No, no. I repressed the thought. If I think it, it becomes real. What if they can read my thoughts? The concept of two unblinking eyes began to take shape. If I think it, it becomes real. And yet, everything was fucking perfect, but something was wrong. Something had to be. I had to be prepared for the bad. It haunted me. At night, snuggling with my pets, it would keep my brain ticking. It would tip my cup of tea. The sound sending my pets in a startled frenzy. The darting eyes at the fuel tank when I would be in space flying a fighter jet from one of the Star Wars movies. The sudden power outage in one of my communes. The laugh that would answer when I tried to think the thoughts away. If I think it, it becomes real.

I met her that evening. Swivelling to catch my tea before it spilled once again. Startled. She was there. She was *real*. She felt familiar, her hair, something in the way she moved. The uncanny feeling of staring into a mirror. I tried to catch a snippet of her, I really did. But her legs, or was it the idea of her legs? They would break into a sprint before I could catch her.

I leapt out of my bed. I had super speed. I would catch her. If I think it, it becomes real. That's how it's always been, right? And yet when I found myself back in the syrup sea world, my fingers brushing her hair, she disappeared. Her laughter ringing out from space. I teleported to the empty vacuum, gravity defying arms grabbing the nothingness as she dematerialised in front of me. On Earth I chased her from Kenya to Japan. Snagging her shirt, just to have her duck out of sight. On the moon she waited for me to get just close enough, her damning laughter trailing like wisps. That time she ran right through me. I willed it. I thought it. I would catch her. Each new world, each new star over the atmosphere. She ducked out of sight, evaded every attack. I used a net once. She once plunged inside a dark hole, I imagined it constricting her, only for her to sidestep once I began to relax. She once stood still beneath the sea, her face almost illuminated by fireflies. I submerged and she was gone. I tried all manner of trap and trick, but I always knew how she'd escape, and so she did. It felt like we had travelled non-reality into a spiral. A never ending, nonsensical, purposeless spiral. Wait, that's familiar…

If it had been thousands of light years who could say, it dawned on me. I could give up. I visualised the all-seeing tree, the powdered diamond soil. I could just give up. And then, that day I finally did. I sat down, looked at the cosmos above and felt like I was seeing the world for the first time. My thoughts blowing through each powdered speck into the all-encompassing syrup sea. The mechanic thrum clearing my mind. Giving up had never felt so easy.

The next time I see a wet patch in the ceiling or whatever other thing sets her off running, I will chase her again. But for now: refuge, respite, a break from the madness.

OUR AUTHORS—

Adam Webber is a British Peruvian writer raised in Mexico City now living in the UK. He started writing a bit of poetry at a young age, but what really got him into writing was a fantasy book he wrote when 15. Since then, he started writing in all kinds of genres and formats. Only recently has he been confident enough with his work to start trying for publication. He has used writing to help him get out of different instances of mental health issues but through this he has been able to re-evaluate and better his writing.

Aisla McKenzie is an aspiring writer hailing from North Wales. Enamoured in her youth by the epic rolling landscapes of the Welsh countryside, then combined with an inspiration fuelled by works such as Ovid's Metamorphoses and Dante's Divine Comedy, her work seeks to explore and redefine myth and fantasy. Her writing attempts to imitate the voices of the ancient storytellers whose oral traditions kept mythology alive through the ages.

Alice May Cunningham is a nineteen year old writer from rural Wales studying English Literature with creative writing. She incorporates her love for the natural world into her poetry and is greatly inspired by folk music, spirituality and folklore. Her love for these topics emerged as a result of growing up in the beautiful Welsh countryside, where the overstimulation of the outside world felt very far away. In the short time she has been at UEA she has been enjoying broadening her literary horizons through reading course texts and other students' work.

Amber Juncal is a queer, British Pakistani Londoner who writes most things that come to mind in a small, pocket-sized notebook that never leaves their side. The few ideas that make it beyond the notebook tend to explore themes of identity, ancestry, and life's many changes and obstacles. Alongside their writing, they also like to draw (mostly stick-men), paint, cut and stick (mostly clippings from free newspapers on the tube) to better understand their own writing.

André Hughes is a dyslexic student of English Literature with Creative Writing at the University of East Anglia. His experimental writing has been published as part of Volume 5 of *Masked Writings/Historias Desconfinades;* a year-long translation and creative writing collaboration with the Universidad de Alcalá, exploring life in a global pandemic. He enjoys the possibilities of blending prose and poetry forms, mixed styles, memory, consciousness, emotion, and the connection between writing and music. In his free time, André enjoys mountain walking, running, food, reading, and travel.

Barnaby Hill is a second-year student originally hailing from North Yorkshire. His work revolves around a fascination for the psychological, strange and synaesthetic, often through a queer lens. He's had previous work published by The 6ress, Handwritten &co, Gypsophila Magazine and UEA's very own creative writing society. If you ever need to find him, he's probably in one of Norwich's many coffee shops, hidden in the corner.

Cat Faux is a final year creative writing student who specialises in poetry. Taking an interest in contemporary poetry during her second year of study, she mainly writes in ways that twist traditional form into something new and exciting, for example this specular poem—a poem that reverses in on itself. Having done some work writing alongside visual art, Cat intends to focus on multimedia projects after her degree and is hoping to be able to work alongside other creatives as well as publish more of her writing.

Cathy Sole studies Creative Writing and Drama at UEA. Though primarily a prose writer, she has written several scripts, screenplays, and poems. In 2021, Cathy completed a Breakthrough Novel Writing course with Curtis Brown Literary Agency, designed to help writers from low-income backgrounds publish their first novel. Her novel (working title Beach Fags) awarded her a spot at a writer's lodge in France where she completed her first draft. Inspired by the likes of Roddy Doyle and Irvine Welsh, Cathy is interested in the grittier side of life, and explores poverty and misogyny in rural settings.

Charlotte Bouilloux is a 21-year-old queer poet and student of English literature and creative writing. Their creative practice mainly lies in confessional poetry where they share musings about love, identity, and their experience with mental illness. Her work has been published in various zines and independent presses such as Good Press, Tale Care zine and Doghouse Press.

Chris Bowler (He/Him) is a writer based in Norwich, who writes mostly poetry, although he is occasionally tempted by a short story. His poetry is mostly surreal and lyrical, without a plot or narrative, relying on a collage of images to tie the poems together. He is interested in conveying emotions through abstract metaphor, and he enjoys using a mixture of natural and sensory imagery. Most of his poems are internally focused, but he has been exploring other themes recently, such as portrait poems and persona poetry.

Daisy Campbell is a third-year English Literature with Creative Writing student. She is interested in poetry which experiments with formal conventions, ekphrasis as a means of translation, and the ethical possibilities and responsibilities of literature.

Denise Monroe is a third year UG on the English Literature and Creative Writing course. She came to university late in life, and has worked previously as a model, assistant film director, mother and massage therapist. Writing will be her next job. Denise likes to write about the small incidence in life that make us the people we become. 'Hanging On' is an extract from her creative writing dissertation and may be the start of a larger piece when she starts the MA in Creative Writing at UEA next year. Unless she starts something completely new, that is.

Diva Hemawani is a prose fiction writer from Jakarta, Indonesia who is currently based in Norwich. They have been writing on and off for over a decade but decided to commit to their craft shortly before coming to UEA to study Creative Writing and English Literature. They draw inspiration from a variety of sources, most notably music (playlists are an essential part of their works in progress!) and random (yet frequent) musings at the most ungodly hours.

Elena Rodgers is a final year undergraduate English Literature student. Through jarring reality and fantasy, her fiction aims to challenge the preconceived ideas about life and literature, exposing what lurks under the performative notion of identity. Throughout her four years at UEA, Elena has written multiple articles for Venue and has been President of Baseball and Softball for the past two years. When she is not writing, you will find her reading, watching films or thinking about what she is going to write next.

Elizabeth Yew (She/They) writes under the nickname "Liz Yew" and has had poems published physically and digitally since she began focusing on writing poetry. Liz grew up in Hong Kong and is now working through a BA in English literature and creative writing in the UK. She never understood poetry growing up, but since discovering Sylvia Plath's work, their own collection of depressing and reflective poetry, along with occasionally cheerful ones, quickly grew. However, being away from home does mean missing her dogs, which they compensate for with her newfound hobby of crocheting.

Ella Pamment is a lover of all things creative, wonderful, and weird. If you ever wondered what type of kitchen utensil you would be—Ella would undoubtedly have the answer! New Address Book, inspired by her frequent moves as a child, captures village life and the unavoidable humorous characters within it. At eighteen, Ella became a self-published author, began writing articles, and is currently studying for her Bachelors in English Literature and Creative Writing. Ella's writing style developed into 'out of the box' forms, leaving her readers laughing, laid-back and well acquainted with the original quirks she brings to literature.

Ellen Newall is a 21 year old writer from West London. They mainly write prose fiction however they have started to dabble with poetry. They are most fond of writing in the horror genre as they are a massive fan of films such as The Babadook and Midsommar.

Emma McDonald is a first year English Literature with Creative Writing BA student, who has lived in both Britain and Switzerland. She primarily writes short fiction and poetry and has recently been using her work to explore geography, grief, culture, liminality and unexpected symbolism as well as the complexities within seemingly mundane relationships. Her collection of poems Seasalt Footsteps aims to provide an emotional insight into the loneliness of grief and how memory tied to place can be both restricting and freeing.

Ersi Zevgoli is a third-year Creative Writing student who is still figuring out how to be Greek in the UK. She runs mostly on words, black coffee, and late-night confessional chats that end in tight hugs. You can find her blowing off steam in the gym, laughing too loudly at the pub, or slaying monsters with her mates at her regular Sunday Dungeons and Dragons session.

Esther Jardine is a drama and English student with an enduring love of poetry. As a child, she discovered a love for stories (and musicals!) and started writing through her diaries. Since then, she has cultivated her interest in different forms of poetry and is drawn to rhyme and rhythm. Esther grew up on a Scottish island and, like other Scottish and Irish poets, is interested in the natural world around us as well as the people in it. She attended an international school abroad and is interested in place and community as well as individual perspectives.

Eve Colabella is a first-year English Literature with Creative Writing student, who, although eager to explore many different forms of writing during her studies, finds that poetry comes the most naturally to her. In the majority of her poetry, she attempts an honest approach to writing, drawing on personal experiences and real emotions to create work that feels raw and genuine, especially through her very specific choices of imagery.

Fin Doktor is a writer whose love of storytelling has lasted as long as he can remember. Fin was born and raised in Norfolk, though has also spent time living in Devon where he studied history and international relations before returning to seriously pursue creative writing. His stories, which often blur the line between the real and the extraordinary, frequently deal with vital and sometimes challenging questions of identity, ego, and alienation. He hopes soon to be able to complete his first collection of short stories, provided he can be convinced of the right place to put that final full stop.

Freya Beth Calcluth is currently a first year Creative Writing and English Literature student, prioritising prose and poetry that can be found on her Instagram *@writtenbyfreya*. Her poetry often consists of themes of yearning or wistfulness, with imagery often inspired by nature and artwork. In terms of prose, she is consistently creating her own worlds inside her head, with only some managing to flow out of her and get written down on paper.

Georgia Greetham is a writer living in Norwich, England. She works as the Vice President for Egg Box Publishing and is a third year English Literature with Creative Writing Student at the University of East Anglia. She has also worked as a submissions volunteer for Boiler House Press and is currently the Social Media Manager for Mausoleum Press.

Grace Bartle is a second year, Drama and Creative Writing student. She comes from a large blended family which has provided extensive inspiration for her writing. (Some of those such pieces would lead to severe conflict if they were ever published.) She has enjoyed writing from a young age, and her work often explores childhood experiences and the topic of growing older. (She claims that this stems from being inconsolable after reading that when Jackie Paper grew up, he stopped playing with Puff the Magic Dragon.) Grace doesn't believe we should ever stop playing with dragons… it makes for great writing.

Ingrid Jensen

Jennifer Shen is a third year visiting student at University of East Anglia. She studies English and creative writing. She devotes a lot of her free time to writing different kinds of poetry and is still exploring who she is as a poet.

Jessica Blissitt is a second year Creative Writing student, and 'The Chicken Dance' is her first published short story. Jess currently enjoys reading and writing Greek Mythology re-writes, like Madeline Miller's Circe or Claire Heywood's Daughters of Sparta. The 'Chicken Dance' was prompted from a disaster date her friend had been on earlier this year, which inspired her to write her own feminist re-write of this story- with a twist! Although she is still a novice writer, Jess continues to write experimental short stories during her semester abroad in America.

Julian Beacom is passionate about writing from the heart and conveying a variety of messages through his storytelling. He was drawn to Creative Writing from an early age and has always sought to create and explore a variety of themes and fantastical worlds through his work.

Kathy Floyd is a Norfolk born and bred writer of fiction, creative nonfiction, complaint correspondence and to-do lists. Like Kit de Waal, she arrived late in life to the creative writing party. She echoes de Waals contention that the publishing industry needs to place more worth on the diversity of writing from under-represented communities if literature is to expand beyond the metropolitan elite. Having religiously followed her nan's advice from forty-odd years ago to 'keep on a troshin no matter what,' she's delighted to be offered a place on the UEAs Biography and Creative Nonfiction MA.

Kyle Wakefield has made it their life's mission to fill the Gothic romance genre with gay and trans people. UEA has taught them the virtues of editing, but their heart belongs to running on sentences and layering metaphors like they're getting paid by the word. When they say they've got the spirit of an 18th century romanticist, they don't mean the Poet-Laureate-to-the-King kind so much as the lying-in-bed-at-noon, coughing-blood-into-a-handkerchief kind. They've got 'Daywalker' tattooed across their chest and they probably have scurvy.

Kyleigh Taylor is a 20-year-old writer studying Creative Writing at UEA as an international student from America. They currently focus on poetry and abstract and surrealism fiction and run an independent critique-based writing workshop.

Laurel Brown is a young writer originally from Bedfordshire but currently lives in Norwich. When she is not writing she spends most of her time reading and watching movies. She is a self proclaimed horror fan which is shown within her writing. She writes short stories of horror, psychological thriller and romance, whilst occasionally dabbling in poetry. She is currently working towards writing her first novel.

Lidia Lassed, 21, is a French and Algerian student and a beginner in creative writing. Lidia has always enjoyed writing to express herself, especially through poetry and fiction. She usually writes about what she feels in the moment but prefers general themes common to many people to give a critical view of the world. She is always questioning herself and believes that nothing can be taken for granted in an ever-changing world, so she is constantly looking for new ways to write. Her main interests are the place of multi-identity in society, racism and self-acceptance.

Lily Fitzgerald is a young poet who often writes in a confessional style and is particularly drawn to portraying moments of emotional intensity where finding the right words can be hard. Although personal experience plays a large role within Lily's works, some of her other poetry concerns the wider female experience drawing on more universal themes of loss, identity and womanhood. This is her first published poem and she strives to produce further works as she enters her third year at university.

Lucy Cundill is a poet living in Norwich, England, where she studies English Literature and Creative Writing at the University of East Anglia. She works as Editor In Chief at Mausoleum Press, the poetry press she set up and runs, and as a Poetry Reader at Patchwork Lit Mag. Her work has been published in publications such as, Full House Literary Magazine, Bandit Fiction, Concrete, the Life Lines zine, and the UEA Undergraduate Creative Writing Anthology. Her work, social media links, and further information can be found at futiledevicez.carrd.co.

Lucy McEleney is a poet and scriptwriter who enjoys exploring the themes of love, religion, and betrayal in her writing, frequently focusing on misogyny and the female voice in order to analyse women's place in our society. She began writing poetry at the age of fourteen, posting her work online via her blog, and still continues to share her creative endeavours through Wordpress, as well as her Instagram *@lucymariepoetry*. She hopes to pursue her passion for screenwriting, whilst also nurturing her love and appreciation for poetry at every possible opportunity.

Maddy Hadwin Donnelly is a third year English Literature with Creative Writing student. After writing her first novel, a piece of dystopian YA fiction, at age fifteen, Maddy has gone on to write another novel, as well as a number of short stories. Influenced by writers such as Miranda July and Katherine Heiny, Maddy's character-driven pieces primarily explore how her characters navigate—often troubled—familial and romantic relationships. In September, following the completion of her undergraduate degree, Maddy will be moving to London to begin her master's degree in Creative and Life Writing at Goldsmiths, University of London.

Magda de Soissons-Page is a third year English and Creative Writing student at UEA. She writes mostly poetry, but occasionally short stories. She has recently been focussing on a collection of sonnets for her dissertation titled Figures from a Lone Bench. Much of her work focusses on animals and the climate in response to the ongoing climate crisis, but also aims to capture moments and feelings in text for preservation of memories for herself and her loved ones.

Maya Elphick is a writer, poet and activist based in Norfolk. In 2019, her debut collection of poetry, White Moth, was published and she has since been featured in six further anthologies exploring current issues from mental health awareness to climate change and sustainability. Maya is currently studying English Literature with Creative Writing at the University of East Anglia.

Megan Dennison, with her love for the short form, is working on a collection of stories that explore the interiority of women's experiences through the lens of religion, femininity and mental health, to which 'The Yellow Room' belongs. She was also published in last year's undergraduate anthology, Under & Over. One half of the London-based duo Own Time, Megan is a songwriter and musician collaborating on their first studio album.

Mia Galanti is a first year English Literature with Creative Writing student. She likes cats, convoluted metaphors and writing about complicated relationship dynamics. Earlier this year she released a play 'Bus Stops' with Audible involving both convoluted metaphors and complicated relationship dynamics (but unfortunately no cats). She is a big believer in run-on sentences and excessive em dash usage, and wouldn't know succinctness if it hit her over the head.

Mica Magsanoc is a 3rd year English Literature with Creative Writing student from the Philippines. Her writing experience includes four years in her high school publication, attending a creative writing summer program at Columbia University, and facilitating writing workshops for kids. Last 2021, she co-authored and edited a Philippine publication titled Fearless Filipinas: *12 Women Who Dared to Be Different*.

Oliver Briggs is in his final year at UEA, studying English Literature and Creative Writing. He was born in London, and lives there whilst not at university. Trips to Scotland and Devon whilst growing up gave him a long-standing interest in historical fiction. Much of his writing combines pseudo-pastoral communities with dark comedy, and he believes this story to be a successful weaving of these themes. Oliver's favourite books include Of Mice And Men by John Steinbeck and Jonathan Strange & Mr Norrell by Susanna Clarke. This is the first time a piece of Oliver's writing has been published—so far.

Paloma Parás was born in México and is a third year Creative Writing student at the University of East Anglia. She is currently interested in examining ideas of nostalgia and loss; what the body and mind hold onto once a thing is gone or in the past. In the future she hopes to explore themes of cultural identity in changing settings.

Robbie Tyler has experimented with all kinds of writing, but largely works on screenplays. The ex-chef has a taste for drama, dark comedy, and anything with a unique voice. Robbie intends to pursue a career in the TV/streaming industry post-graduation. As a poet, he describes himself as optimistic, laconic, and self-aware.

Rowena Price is a third year English Literature and Creative Writing student, soup-maker and folklore fanatic. She loves the ability of poetry to transform small, everyday moments, and this is what she hopes to achieve in her own work.

Seb Lloyd is a 3rd year English Literature and Creative Writing student who has written for Concrete, Livewire1350 and the UG Anthology in his time at UEA. He is currently working on his Creative Writing Dissertation in Poetry and has performed his poetry extensively since 2017.

Sophie Wallwin is a final year English Literature and Creative Writing student who enjoys working openly across forms. In her script and prose, she writes of the tangled nature of various human relationships, often searching for softness in conflict, whereas in poetry she is often drawn to the natural world, capturing and appreciating its grounding and remedial powers. In the future, she hopes to experiment with combining various disciplines and looks forward to connecting the different threads of her writing in new and energising ways.

Synne Solbrekken is a final year English Lit and Creative Writing student from Norway. Her main focus throughout her degree has been prose but her style is quite poetic. She likes to play with language and meaning and tries to take advantage of the polysemy of English words. English being her second language, she finds herself gravitating towards more accessible poetry but explores the layers of simple yet effective imagery.

Thomas Smith is a prose and screen writer from Lincolnshire. His main style would be minimalist contemporary fiction, choosing to focus on character and relationships, whether that be related to friendship, romance or rivalry (or sometimes all three!). Finishing off his first novel and creating this piece has helped him create a style which he finds conveys all those themes and is excited to share it with the world.

Tianyu Zhou was born and raised in Beijing, China. She is doing a degree on English with creative writing at UEA. In her writings, she likes to explore the power of things that remained unseen or unsaid. The idea of this story came to her when she was taking a walk around the lake on campus for the first time.

Victoria Her is a final year English Literature with Creative Writing undergraduate at the University of East Anglia. At fifteen, she wrote and self-published her first book on French dessert and pastry. A French national of Dutch and Ukrainian origin, she grew up in rural Thailand, where she was exposed to different oral storytelling, folklore and philosophies which inform her writing. Her neurodivergence is reflected in her writing, combining fantastical worlds and the human psyche. As a passionate advocate for mental health destigmatization and promoting accessibility in literature, her writing

WITH THANKS TO—

The Editing Team:
Oliver Hancock Editor-in-Chief
Maddy Hadwin Donnelly assisting Editor in Chief
Kate Oskirko assisting Editor-in-Chief
Isabel Murphy assisting Editor-in-Chief
Elizabeth Yew assisting Editor-in-Chief

Sadie Harte
Helena Keys
Rosie Kyrin-White
Clea Licht
Mica Magsanoc
Jennifer Shen

The 2022 Egg Box Committee:
Oliver Hancock President
Georgia Greetham Vice-President
Evie Pledger Treasurer
Lily Boag Secretary
Rebekah Philipson Events Officer
Kate Oskirko Social Secretary
Beth Lane Equality & Diversity Officer
Isabel Murphy Health & Safety Officer
Maddy Hadwin Donnelly Union Council Representative
Elizabeth Yew First Year Representative

UNDERGROUND

First published by Egg Box Publishing in 2022
Part of UEA Publishing Project Ltd
International ©2022 retained by individual authors
A CIO record of this book is available from the
British Library

This book is sold subject to the condition that
it shall not, by way of trade or otherwise, be lent,
resold, hired out, stored in a retrieval system,
or otherwise circulated without the publisher's prior
consent in any form of binding or cover other than
that in which it is published and without a similar
condition including the condition being imposed
on the subsequent purchaser.

Underground is typeset in Adobe Garamond Pro
Cover design and type setting by Anna Brewster
Printed and bound in the UK by Imprint Digital
Distributed by NBN International

ISBN: 978-1-913861-83-4

Egg Box Instagram:
@theeggbox

UEA UNDERGRADUATE ANTHOLOGY
2021-2022